theatre & feminism

Theatre&
Series Standing Order ISBN 978–0–230–20327–3

You can receive future titles in this series as they are published by placing a standing order. Please contact your bookseller or, in case of difficulty, write to us at the address below with your name and address, the title of the series and the ISBN quoted above.

Customer Services Department, Macmillan Distribution Ltd, Houndmills, Basingstoke, Hampshire, RG21 6XS, UK

theatre &
feminism

Kim Solga

First published 2016 by
PALGRAVE

Red Globe Press in the UK is an imprint of Springer Nature Limited,
registered in England, company number 785998, of 4 Crinan Street, London,
N1 9XW.

Palgrave Macmillan in the US is a division of St Martin's Press LLC,
175 Fifth Avenue, New York, NY 10010.

Red Globe Press is a global imprint of the above companies and is
represented throughout the world.

Red Globe Press® is a registered trademark in the United States, the United
Kingdom, Europe and other countries.

ISBN 978–1–137–46300–5

This book is printed on paper suitable for recycling and made from fully
managed and sustained forest sources. Logging, pulping and manufacturing
processes are expected to conform to the environmental regulations of the
country of origin.

A catalogue record for this book is available from the British Library.

A catalog record for this book is available from the Library of Congress.

contents

T he theatre is everywhere, from entertainment districts to the fringes, from the rituals of government to the ceremony of the courtroom, from the spectacle of the sporting arena to the theatres of war. Across these many forms stretches a theatrical continuum through which cultures both assert and question themselves.

Theatre has been around for thousands of years, and the ways we study it have changed decisively. It's no longer enough to limit our attention to the canon of Western dramatic literature. Theatre has taken its place within a broad spectrum of performance, connecting it with the wider forces of ritual and revolt that thread through so many spheres of human culture. In turn, this has helped make connections across disciplines; over the past 50 years, theatre and performance have been deployed as key metaphors and practices with which to rethink gender, economics, war, language, the fine arts, culture and one's sense of self.

Theatre & is a long series of short books which hopes to capture the restless interdisciplinary energy of theatre and performance. Each book explores connections between theatre and some aspect of the wider world, asking how the theatre might illuminate the world and how the world might illuminate the theatre. Each book is written by a leading theatre scholar and represents the cutting edge of critical thinking in the discipline.

We have been mindful, however, that the philosophical and theoretical complexity of much contemporary academic writing can act as a barrier to a wider readership. A key aim for these books is that they should all be readable in one sitting by anyone with a curiosity about the subject. The books are challenging, pugnacious, visionary sometimes and, above all, clear. We hope you enjoy them.

Jen Harvie and Dan Rebellato

theatre & feminism

Introduction

Theatre & Feminism tells the story of the movement known as feminist performance theory and criticism, the lens through which scholars understand theatre and performance practices that take gender difference, and gendered experience, as their primary social and political focus. This story, then, is about women and theatre, women at the theatre and women in and of the theatre; but it is also more than that. Above all, it is about how feminist theatre theory and practice allows us to understand the way *all* gender is constructed and reinforced in performance, for better and for worse, and for all human beings on the planet – be they men, women, transpersons or others. "Feminism" remains a contentious term (more on that in a moment), but for me it is the best and most accurate term to use when thinking about gendered experience from a human rights perspective. Any human being worried about discrimination on the

1

basis of gender or sexual orientation will have some affinity with the term, whether or not they realize it; similarly, this book aims to demonstrate the many ways that feminist scholars and makers of theatre and performance have enabled, and continue to enable, productive discussions about women's (and others') experiences of gender, sexuality, political power and human rights, both on and off the stage.

My version of this story begins in 2005. That August, Jill Dolan – one of my mentors, and the author of the pioneering 1988 book *The Feminist Spectator as Critic* – began writing her popular blog, *The Feminist Spectator*. I spent the spring of that year working on my postdoctoral research with Jill in the Performance as a Public Practice programme at the University of Texas, Austin. The lessons of *her* feminist practice – as a scholar, a teacher and a spectator to the many shows we watched together – stayed with me after I returned to Canada, thickening and re-politicizing my own feminist archive and shaping the way I tackled my first academic job. Thanks to Jill's revitalization of the "Feminist Spectator" brand on her blog, 2005 became indelibly linked in my imagination with its origins in her 1988 book, and the connection prompted me to think about the trajectory feminist performance theory and criticism had taken over the intervening 17 years. Was the movement that had so fully shaped my own research, teaching, theatrical tastes and political imagination now properly "history"? If it was "history" and yet remained urgently relevant to me, what was different about it today, and what had *not* changed? Given Dolan's deliberate choice to turn her acclaimed book into a blog directed at a public audience, could we argue that feminist performance criticism, like so much contemporary feminism, had gone "mainstream," become the norm or status quo rather than a movement pushing in from the margins? If that was indeed the case, why should we still keep talking about it?

These are the questions that have framed my engagement with feminist performance scholarship over the last few years, and that remind me never to take the value and impact of my commitment to feminist critique for granted. The research questions that drive this book embed these questions, but also extend them. First, I ask: what did feminist performance theory and criticism aim to achieve when it broke onto the critical scene in the 1970s and 1980s, and how did it go about the task? What critical strategies in use then are still in use now, and what new critical strategies have feminist scholars and makers of theatre and performance adopted, and adapted, as the political landscape has shifted between then and now? Second, I ask: why is this form of criticism still important – indeed, to my mind, still *vital* – for students, scholars and makers of theatre today? How have shifts over time in the popular meaning of the label "feminist" affected the ways we might perceive theatre and performance work that openly identifies as such – or that *refuses* to identify as such? How might fresh work by feminist scholars and makers today help us to understand the limitations, even the dangers, of imagining that we now live in a "post-feminist" age?

The bulk of this book is devoted to exploring the history of feminist performance theory and criticism alongside its lively contemporary afterlife. In three main sections I examine three central frameworks that feminist scholars and makers have used to unpack the way gendered experiences are both represented on stage and also manufactured in performance in order to seem "given" or "natural" both on stage and in the world outside the theatre. Each section – "looking/watching/spectating"; "being versus acting"; and "hope and loss" – discusses influential theoretical texts, engages with critical debates, and features a very recent case study that demonstrates how the strategies discussed in the section can be applied to work being made and shown in theatres right now. In my conclusion I look at recent work by Peggy Shaw – arguably the most influential Anglophone feminist performer of the late twentieth century – in order to think about what happens to the feminist performance body (the body of the artist as well as the body of the critic) as we all get older in a world where women over a certain age (sadly, about 40) remain pitifully under-represented in public life and especially invisible in Hollywood and on Broadway. Before we reach the shores of these histories, however, I want to spend some time addressing my second research question, and with it those readers who might wonder if "feminism" itself ought not, by now, be history.

Feminism now: the paradox of "post"

I'm writing this book in summer and autumn 2014; for many women (especially white, middle-class women) in the Anglophone West (which broadly includes the US, Canada,

Australia, New Zealand and the UK, as well as South Africa and pockets of Asia), things have never been better. Michelle Obama is First Lady of the United States. Kathleen Wynne, an "out" lesbian, was recently elected premier of my home province of Ontario. The world is mourning the passing of African-American author and activist Maya Angelou, remembering her as one of the most important public figures of the twentieth century. Major TV stars like Lena Dunham (creator, writer and star of the major HBO hit *Girls*) are open, proud feminists, unafraid to speak their minds or their politics in public. In the pop music industry, a hothouse of conservative attitudes about femininity, icons Beyoncé and Taylor Swift have declared themselves feminists too. In the UK, authors Caitlin Moran (*How to Be a Woman*, 2012), Holly Baxter and Rhiannon Lucy Cosslett (*The Vagenda: A Zero Tolerance Guide to the Media*, 2014) are enormously popular as they aim forceful, satirical arrows at the now visibly retrograde social attitudes that continue to get in women's way. Haitian-American writer Roxane Gay addresses the other side of that coin in her new book of essays, *Bad Feminist* (2014), which describes the often-hilarious challenges of living and working as a feminist while also enjoying dating, sex and popular culture. Meanwhile, Laura Bates's *Everyday Sexism* project has gone viral, expanding to multiple countries and attracting more than 200,000 followers on Twitter alone. Women occupy high-profile public roles as doctors, lawyers, professors, engineers and politicians throughout Europe, Asia and the Americas. Many women feel very safe on the streets alone; many women feel able to move through the world as they please. These gains, these freedoms, are what feminism has, for over a hundred years now, been fighting for.

This is the bright, cheerful, front-of-house view. If I glance backstage for a moment, however, the picture darkens. Bates's *Everyday Sexism* project is wildly popular online – but this popularity simply means that many of the virulently sexist attitudes we often ascribe to a pre-feminist past are still alive and well today. Bates has also been the victim of significant trolling (Holman), another regular feature of contemporary life for women in the public sphere. Julia Gillard, the first female prime minister of Australia, was hounded from office in 2013 by a parliament openly hostile to her status as a (married but childless) woman. Michelle Obama is *First Lady*, not President; her husband handily beat Hillary Clinton for the Democratic nomination and, unlike Clinton, was rarely asked about his fashion preferences in the process. Though stars like Dunham are setting bold examples for young women in the media and in Hollywood, only 28 per cent of speaking parts in the top 100 films of 2012 were played by women (Bates 184).

In the theatre industry, the statistics on gender equity are equally troubling. A 2009 study undertaken by Emily Glassberg Sands in the US revealed not only systemic discrimination against women playwrights in that country, but that this discrimination was driven primarily by *female* literary managers and artistic directors (Cohen). Glassberg Sands's work thus exposed the extent to which ingrained biases toward women and their abilities inhere in both men and women in patriarchal societies. In 2006, a similar study on Canadian theatre industry trends revealed that no more than one third of "key positions of creativity and authority," including artistic directorships, roles as directors and published playwrights, were occupied by women (Burton ii). The picture is considerably more grim for non-white women working in the theatre (see Perkins and Richards, and Catanese), TV and film in the Anglosphere; we also need to remember that non-white women face significantly increased hostility and danger compared to white women when out in public, both in democratic states as well as in states where girls and women remain second-class citizens, if citizens at all.

All of which brings us to the paradox of post-feminism. "Post-feminist" is the term some critics use to describe a historical moment (roughly the period after the mid-1980s) in which men and women appeared to have achieved gender equality in the workplace and in the public sphere, and thus in which the original goals of feminist theory and practice appeared redundant. As the quite informative and relatively accurate Wikipedia page for "Postfeminism" puts it, "Postfeminism gives the impression that equality has been achieved and that feminists can now focus on something else entirely." Equality, however, takes many forms, and *in*equality can be insidious in ways that are deeply felt, yet not immediately visible on the surface of our daily experiences. To return to the evidence I cited above: how can women living in post-industrial democracies have attained so much and yet remain, statistically speaking, still so far from their primary goals? If many women *feel*, day-to-day, free and equal, how can it be that a feminist politics they associate with their mothers and grandmothers is not only *not* outmoded but also still necessary?

Feminism, post-feminism and neoliberalism

The British theorist Angela McRobbie offers some helpful explanations for how the paradox of post-feminism emerged over the last three decades, alongside the rise of the political movement known as neoliberalism. According to McRobbie, neoliberalism has made way for extraordinary advances for young women – not as a community, importantly, but as *individuals* who are able to succeed in education and the workplace, advance in their careers, and thus perceive themselves (and *all* women, by extension) as treated fairly and equally. This illusion of gender fairness and equity erases our ability, as individuals, to see problems that still linger in the bigger picture.

In *A Brief History of Neoliberalism*, David Harvey defines "neoliberalism" as the free-market-driven model of governance that "proposes that human well-being can best be advanced by liberating individual entrepreneurial freedoms and skills within an institutional framework characterized by strong private property rights, free markets and free trade" (2). Under neoliberalism, the role of the state is to preserve these rights, markets and trade relationships above all else, valuing "market exchange as 'an ethic in itself, capable of acting as a guide to all human action'" (3). Neoliberalism dictates that government gets "out of our way," leaving individuals free to earn money and advance their careers; these same individuals, supposedly, can then take care of their own – and then everyone, in theory, makes progress and feels better.

If this sounds familiar, it's because neoliberalism has been the prevailing, often unquestioned, political ideology under globalization since at least the late 1970s. The neoliberal model is not new to the late twentieth century, but it became virtually unquestioned among Anglo-European democracies during the parallel leaderships of US president Ronald Reagan and UK prime minister Margaret Thatcher in the 1980s, and it shaped the primary ideology of the UK's "New Labour" movement under Tony Blair in the 1990s and early 2000s. In many countries today – and not just in those typically called "Western" – neoliberalism has come to seem normal, natural and thus not worth questioning; it's just the way things *are*.

McRobbie takes the title of her important 2007 article on feminism's relationship to neoliberalism, "Top Girls?", from Caryl Churchill's landmark 1982 play of the same name. In this play, one of the most important British feminist dramas of the twentieth century, main character Marlene wins a promotion to Managing Director at the "Top Girls" employment agency over her male peer, Howard. Marlene holds her own – and reveals a clear, though basic, feminist politics – in the second act when Howard's wife appears to challenge her right, as a woman, to do the job; when time comes to support other women looking to move out of traditionally gendered jobs and into more challenging work, however, Marlene proves herself every bit as ruthless, and sexist, as a traditional patriarch. Her right-wing, free-market politics are especially visible in her dealings with her sister Joyce and Joyce's – in reality, Marlene's – daughter, Angie, whom she brutally judges as "thick" and unlikely to "make it" in the working world (66). Churchill organizes the play using Brechtian dramaturgy (I'll speak more about feminist performance theory's debt to Brecht in the section titled "Being versus Acting") and plenty of carefully positioned irony in order to critique Marlene's "post-feminist" politics even as she demonstrates how seductive that politics can be.

McRobbie succinctly sums up the broader political strategy that lies behind Marlene's behaviour:

> Within specified social conditions and political constraints, young, increasingly well-educated women, of different ethnic and social backgrounds, now find themselves charged with the requirement that they perform as economically active female citizens. They are invited to recognise themselves as privileged subjects of social change, perhaps they might even be expected to be grateful for the support they have received. ... [The young, well-educated woman] is addressed as though she is already "gender aware" [and] as a result of equal opportunities policies in the education system *and with all of this feminist influence somehow behind her*, she is now pushed firmly in the direction of independence and self reliance. ... These female individualisation

      processes *require that young women become impor-*
tant to themselves. (722–3, my emphasis)

For women like Marlene in *Top Girls*, the post-feminist neoliberal reality is an attractive one. But Marlene's very success, McRobbie argues, is predicated "on condition that feminism fades away" (720) – that is, on the condition that her perception of her own equality *erases* the need for her to stand up on behalf of women like Joyce, Angie and all those at her employment agency who simply want what she already takes for granted.

    It's important to note that this pervasive, effective illusion that our feminist job is done is not a by-product of neoliberalism's investment in free markets as a source of ethical progress; in fact, the illusion that *your* good fortune is, or at least can be, *every woman's* good fortune is deliberately cultivated by neoliberal institutions. Women who feel equal may in turn feel no urgent need to mobilize against remaining inequalities, even when those inequalities live startlingly close to home; and because protest and political unrest is considered bad for financial market stability, shutting down a public appetite for feminist protest is considered a "win" for business and the governments that openly support it. As British scholar Elaine Aston concludes, referring to Churchill's play, community-engaged feminism was a primary "casualty of Thatcher's right-wing 'superwoman' – the individual, materially successful woman privileged above any altruistic concern for women's collective welfare" (578).

Of course, not every woman or man who resists the "feminist" label is a Marlene; many of us are politically aware and broadly sympathetic to arguments like McRobbie's, yet are also reticent about using a term that remains clouded by persistent stereotypes of angry, bra-burning man-haters. As I write this in 2014, feminism is having an undisputed moment in the sunshine, but feminists as a group of politically engaged women are still routinely smeared in the media and mocked by commentators on the Right for being angry over "nothing" – for ignoring the basic, simple truth that the battle is over and women "won" (Wente). As Roxane Gay counters in *Bad Feminist*, though:

> Pointing out the many ways in which misogyny persists and harms women is not anger. Conceding the idea that anger is an inappropriate reaction to the injustice women face backs women into an unfair position. Nor does disagreement mean we are blind to the ways in which progress has been made. Feminists are celebrating our victories and acknowledging our privilege when we have it. We're simply refusing to settle. We're refusing to forget how much work there is yet to be done. (102)

Gay is interested in the many ways feminist politics get articulated across the political spectrum today, both by those who identify with the "feminist" label and by those who do not. In the field of feminist performance theory, Elaine Aston has recently made the provocative claim that an uncertain feeling about the word "feminism" has been a defining feature of women's playwriting in the UK for some time ("Feeling the Loss of Feminism"), including in the landmark work of Sarah Kane. Many women playwrights, as well as younger, committed feminist scholars like Gay, share popular concerns about the way "feminism" *as a marker of identity* resonates both positively and negatively for different men and women – but, importantly, that *does not mean* they choose to disown the term. Instead, they push its boundaries by critically investigating its meanings and impacts.

American performance scholar Jessica Pabón has discovered in her fieldwork in Chile how complicated the practice of feminism can be for young performance artists in South America today. Working with women graffiti artists (*graffiteras*), Pabón discovered among them a strong, shared feminist ethic but a refusal to adopt the label. The artists she studied saw "feminism" as an overtly political practice, not an artistic one, and did not want to be aligned to the specific connotations it carries in Chile. (Chile, though currently a democracy, has a recent history of extreme political instability and government-sponsored genocide.) Nevertheless, Pabón highlights these artists' affinity to feminism by examining their creation of supportive women's communities, including the sharing of child-rearing; by exploring the ways in which they take up public space, as women, in what is traditionally considered a man's field; and by theorizing the ways in which their refusal of the feminist label might prompt scholars to think again about how that label

13

can sometimes be unhelpfully limiting for women artists, especially in fraught political contexts. "[F]eminism," Pabón concludes of the *graffiteras* in her study, "is what [these women] *do*, not how they identify" (91, my emphasis).

Post-feminism is a seductive idea in theory, but it is not (at least, not yet) a reality in practice. As I have argued in this introductory section, many more women than we might, individually, be able to imagine are still struggling uphill toward the kind of privileges a minority of us enjoy. And because many more women are "doing" feminism than merely identifying with it, we need to pay attention to feminist *practice* as well as feminist ideology in order to account for their labour and their successes. Feminist performance theory and criticism developed in the later twentieth century in order to do just that.

Three ways to understand a movement

The next part of this book explores the history of feminist performance theory and criticism in depth. This part is divided into three sections, in which I focus my discussion around three different critical debates that have been of special importance to feminist performance theorists, especially those working in the UK, the US and Canada over the last several decades. First, I'll look at how feminist performance theory emerged in part from a feminist impulse in film theory to theorize the spectator's gaze, and I'll consider three landmark early works by Jill Dolan, Peggy Phelan and Elin Diamond that together develop a specifically feminist theory of *looking* at the theatre. Second, I'll examine the debate over stage realism that developed as part of feminist performance theory's debt to Bertolt Brecht; here, I'll talk about Judith Butler's influence on the field, and especially on its resistance to theatrical illusion, via her influential theory of gender as social performance. Finally, I'll consider how both of these earlier debates – over the nature of feminist spectatorship on one hand, and over the politics of realism on the other – have informed contemporary feminist work on the theatre as a place to experience and explore political *feelings*, especially feelings of hope (for a better, more gender-equal world), as well as feelings of loss (for the currency of feminism itself, and its political force).

Of course the divisions, as well as the examples and case studies, I have chosen here are necessarily personal and idiosyncratic; this book can offer only one of many potential histories of feminist performance theory and criticism. As a committed feminist theatre scholar, educated in the geographical region known as the Anglophone West, who came of age while some of the most important work in the field was being discussed, I am proud to tell this story – but I cannot pretend it is definitive. Although I write this book as an individual, I hope that I can do justice to the collaborative nature of the feminist performance project; to that end I try to highlight whenever possible the connections between scholars, and among scholars and artists, that enabled certain arguments in feminist performance circles to take on particular social and political force, and to propel certain kinds of change. As my history unfolds I pay particular attention to critical books and articles and offer one major theatrical case study per section, but I also mention important feminist plays and performance events along the way.

Looking/watching/spectating

The year 1988–89 was a watershed for feminist performance theory and criticism. It saw the publication of Sue-Ellen Case's *Feminism and Theatre*, the first book to craft a feminist theatre history (and to examine key moments in theatre history from a plainly feminist point of view), Lynda Hart's edited collection *Making A Spectacle: Feminist Essays on Contemporary Women's Theatre*, as well as Jill Dolan's *The Feminist Spectator as Critic*, the first book to account self-reflexively for the work of feminist performance scholars through the 1970s and 1980s and to advance a comprehensive theory of feminist theatrical viewing. Meanwhile, in its first issue of that year, *TDR (The Drama Review)* showcased a brace of feminist work, including an article on and an interview with performance artists Rachel Rosenthal (see Lampe) and Karen Finley, respectively, as well as two now-canonical essays. The first of those was Peggy Phelan's "Feminist Theory, Poststructuralism, and Performance," which prefigured her landmark work on feminist performance and the politics of visibility in *Unmarked: The Politics of Performance* (1993). The second was Elin Diamond's "Brechtian Theory/ Feminist Theory: Toward a Gestic Feminist Criticism," arguably the single most influential piece of writing in the feminist performance canon, and one of several essays and book chapters in which feminist critics in the late 1980s and early 1990s repurposed the theory of mid-century German director and playwright Bertolt Brecht for feminist ends.

How did feminist performance scholarship arrive at this vanguard moment? Dolan, Case, Hart, Phelan and Diamond did not create their texts in isolation; they were part of a larger community of thinkers, both men and women, who throughout the 1980s shared ideas and material, edited one another's writing in scholarly journals (such as the pioneering *Women & Performance*), gathered to talk to one another at conferences and in working groups (such as at the Women and Theatre group, now part of the Association for Theatre in Higher Education [ATHE]) and shared the pleasures of viewing and celebrating brand new performance and live art at lower Manhattan's WOW Café (home of Split Britches, The Five Lesbian Brothers, Holly Hughes, Carmelita Tropicana and other iconic practitioners). The acknowledgements pages of Dolan's book, and of Diamond's 1997 *Unmaking Mimesis*, go a long way towards crafting a genealogy of the hothouse period of the 1980s and early 1990s, offering historians of feminist performance some insight into the kinship and professional networks that feminists built to sustain their writing and thinking during that crucial time.

Through the mid-1980s, as Case and Dolan would have been preparing their book manuscripts, Case was also an editor at *Theatre Journal*, which along with *TDR* was (and is) one of the most influential scholarly journals in the larger fields of theatre and performance studies. In 1990 Case published *Performing Feminisms: Feminist Critical Theory and Theatre*, collecting together 20 essays that she and

Timothy Murray, another former *TJ* editor, had seen into print between 1984 and 1989 as part of a deliberate push to foreground feminist theory and critique in *TJ*'s pages (1). The resulting anthology features work by Diamond, Dolan, Jeanie Forte, Vivian Patraka, Janelle Reinelt, Teresa de Lauretis, Glenda Dickerson, Judith Butler and a host of other influential women academics in both theatre and film studies. By 1993, new books by Lizbeth Goodman in the UK (*Contemporary Feminist Theatres: To Each Her Own*), Phelan in the US (*Unmarked*) and Phelan with Hart (*Acting Out: Feminist Performances*) had confirmed feminist performance criticism's significance, as well as its status as a theoretically rigorous discipline that drew its ideological and political force from cultural materialism (particularly in the UK context), feminist film theory (especially in the US), and psychoanalytic theory.

Theorizing the feminist spectator: Laura Mulvey and Jill Dolan

Cultural materialism refers to the study of the social, political and economic conditions that shape the choices made by individuals in specific real-world contexts, as well as by characters on stage; Freudian and Lacanian psychoanalytic theories, meanwhile, examine how humans become subjects through the acts of looking, watching and desiring what they see. By blending both of these theories with feminist theatrical examples, writers like Dolan, Diamond and Phelan crafted feminist performance theory's core understanding of the gendered nature of the spectator's gaze at the theatre. Importantly, this "gaze" does not simply refer to one individual's act of looking at (or on) the stage; the gaze may be focused through individual viewers' eyes, but it derives from those viewers' unconscious commitment to shared social and cultural expectations about how men and women *should* each appear, act and speak, both on stage and in the world in a given place and time. The gaze is thus one of the means by which, as Michel Foucault argues in *Discipline and Punish: The Birth of the Prison* (1975), human beings police their shared cultural mores in public and maintain the dominant culture's status quo when it comes to sex and gender difference. (Here, by way of a rudimentary example, we might think about times in our lives when we have deliberately chosen to wear clothes or hairstyles typical of our peers, or of the latest trends in magazines, so as not to stand out as "weird" or "unnatural" at school or at work.) In the early pages of *The Feminist Spectator as Critic*, Dolan helpfully explains the relationship between the gaze as a *cultural apparatus*, and the gaze as part of individual spectators' viewing practices:

> Since the resurgence of American feminism in the 1960s, feminist theatre makers and critics have worked to expose the gender-specific nature of theatrical representation, and to radically modify its terms. ... Since it directs its address to a gender-specific spectator, most performance employs culturally determined gender codes that reinforce cultural conditioning. Performance usually addresses the male spectator as an active subject, and encourages him to identify with the male hero

in the narrative. The same representations tend to objectify women performers and female spectators as passive, invisible, unspoken subjects. (1–2)

Dolan's most important claim here — that theatre "directs its address to a gender specific spectator" — derives from her reading of Laura Mulvey's game-changing essay "Visual Pleasure and Narrative Cinema," published in the journal *Screen* in 1975. Mulvey's work is emblematic of the psychoanalysis-inflected film criticism of its moment, and it explains how twentieth-century Hollywood cinema invites male spectators to look to female characters on screen as both erotic objects of desire *and* affirmations of their own idealized masculine selves. Building on the Freudian concept of *scopophilia*, which refers to a fascination with looking at others in a "controlling and curious" way (Freud 157; Mulvey 8), Mulvey writes:

> In a world ordered by sexual imbalance, pleasure in looking has been split between active/male and passive/female. The determining male gaze projects its phantasy on to the female figure which is styled accordingly. In their traditional exhibitionist role women are simultaneously looked at and displayed, with their appearance coded for strong visual and erotic impact so that they can be said to connote *to-be-looked-at-ness*. (11)

As we think about the complex ideas contained in this quotation, it's imperative to recognize Mulvey's "male gaze" not as a physical feature of individual men's bodies, but rather as part of film's material apparatus, its mechanics of image creation. For Mulvey, the gaze is shaped and directed in cinema through the twin technologies of the camera's lens and the film's narrative. In the mid-twentieth-century films that Mulvey uses as examples (including those of Alfred Hitchcock), the camera's lens tends to focus closely on specific parts of women's bodies, which are thereby transformed into fetish objects for the viewer, and it tracks their movements in ominous, suspense-building fashion. The camera directs spectators to watch the film's action through the eyes of its powerful male protagonist; it follows the female character and implies both her availability and her vulnerability. Meanwhile, in these film's narratives, women characters typically figure as heroines to be saved or antagonists to be punished by those same powerful male leads. Lest Mulvey's claims seem dated, we might consider for a moment the ways in which, for example, the recent Blockbuster *Twilight* films permit male viewers to identify with the anti-heroic Edward but romanticize his lover/prey Bella. Or, we might think of how even the politically progressive and widely acclaimed HBO series *Breaking Bad* cast Anna Gunn's Skyler White as the nagging, hectoring domestic obstacle to Walter White's life-affirming criminal activities. The narrative structures that helped to shape our perception of Skyler also enabled a virulent backlash against both the character and Gunn online – a backlash clearly oblivious to the ways the show's politics of representation had encouraged us to dislike her as a "difficult" wife and mother from the beginning (see Ryan).

Theatre scholars reading important feminist film critics such as Mulvey, Teresa de Lauretis, Mary Ann Doane and others of course realized that film and theatre are very different media: the absolute control over the cinematic gaze maintained by a film's cameras and editing can never be replicated in live performance, where audiences are in theory free to look at any part of the stage or auditorium space at any time. Nevertheless, as Dolan notes in her chapter on the male gaze in *The Feminist Spectator as Critic* (40–58), the theatre's apparatus of representation can also exert covert but stringent controls over the kinds of things audience members are ostensibly free to see. In the modern narrative dramas that have long been canonized as classics, for example, entrances, exits and dialogue are often shaped to encourage particular kinds of views of female characters, especially when those characters are marked by the play as strong, difficult or simply central to the story. Think about the first act of Ibsen's *Hedda Gabler* (1890): we do not meet Hedda until several characters have gossiped about her, priming us to view her through their eyes as a cruel, selfish woman. Or note how Blanche DuBois's sordid history rears up in the middle of Tennessee Williams's *A Streetcar Named Desire* (1947) in order to "explain" her behaviour, encouraging us to see her emotional distress as an illness (and her own fault) rather than as a function of her present situation as a single woman alone, dispossessed and trapped in her sister's home with a violent brother-in-law. This is not to suggest that directors, actors, producers and designers are not able to choose from a host of different approaches to these texts in performance in order to shift, minimize or expose the ways in which narrative structures influence our views of individual stage figures. Regardless of these approaches, however, as Dolan writes, the ideological assumptions that *always* lie behind the shaping of stage images – whether through text, set design, actors' work on characters, lighting, direction and more – inevitably guide our eyes and focus our perceptual faculties (41).

Under such circumstances, where is a woman at the theatre to look? And how might her different *context* for looking – the experience of living in a female body in her culture that she brings with her to the performance – be used to empower other spectators to see, and to question, what can otherwise seem to be no more than "natural" or "inevitable" gender differences on stage? Dolan's book is meant as an activist primer for the viewer who, sitting at the theatre, realizes uncomfortably that her position as a spectator is compromised, pinned between the "unsavoury" options of identifying with objectified women or aligning herself with men who are at best condescendingly heroic and at worst physically violent (2). But the larger question her project poses – of where and how feminists might *look through and at* the apparatus of the "male gaze" in order to expose its ideological workings for the sakes of both men and women – is the one that preoccupied the majority of feminist performance critics through the 1990s.

"Active vanishing": Peggy Phelan
Two other important texts from this period helpfully articulate two major options feminist performance theory

developed for resisting the male gaze and subjecting it to analysis and critique. Following Mulvey and extending her use of Freudian psychoanalysis, Peggy Phelan's *Unmarked: The Politics of Performance* built a theory of radical invisibility for feminist artists and scholars working in live art, photography, film and theatre. In the book's introduction, Phelan explains Jacques Lacan's notion of the phallic function: the idea that men, in Western culture, are accorded the power of the phallus (not a penis, but its symbolic representation, a mark of cultural authority), while women "are" the phallus, the thing men seek to possess in order to make their authority *as men* visible to others (17). Lacan's theory insists on a binary division between men and women, but also describes how this division is not so much biologically innate as it is a function of the way phallic desire, and the accompanying fear that one may lack phallic power (which is a social pressure more than a biological one) trains our vision, requiring us to see certain people as valuable, or not, in certain situations. Phelan argues:

> One term of the binary is marked with value, the other is unmarked. The male is marked with value; the female is unmarked. ... cultural reproduction takes she who is unmarked and re-marks her, rhetorically and imagistically, while he who is marked with value is left unremarked, in discursive paradigms and visual fields. (5)

Man *sees*; woman *is seen*: as gorgeous, too-perfect, flawed; as available for sex; as too smart for her own good or not smart enough; above all, as always second-best. Thus, Phelan concludes, "visibility is a trap" (6) for women on public view, whether that is on the stage or in any other form of "cultural reproduction," from film and theatre to novels and newspaper articles, to dinner parties and public debates.

Phelan's argument here is somewhat controversial. She was writing in the US at a time when public attempts by members of racial and sexual minorities to gain more authority from a still largely white political and economic establishment insisted that the more you were seen and heard, the more likely you were to achieve power. On the contrary, Phelan argued: what matters is *how* you are positioned to be seen and heard, how you occupy (or not) the role scripted for you within a visual field organized by the *powers that see*. The position of power is not the one in front of the camera; it's the one behind the camera. Importantly, Phelan directs her arguments in *Unmarked* at critical race activists as well as feminist activists, noting that the gaze, especially in Europe and the Anglosphere, is never simply male, but also largely white.

To counter this pressure on women (of all racial backgrounds) to be seen in certain ways in cultural representations, Phelan prescribed an "*active* vanishing, a deliberate and conscious refusal to take the payoff of visibility" (19). This "active vanishing" takes many forms in *Unmarked*'s many case studies, but it always includes two important features. First: it is actively *marked as not seen*; it is never simply not there. Second: it forces the viewer, the bearer of the gaze – whether that bearer, in the moment of representation, is a male spectator or a female one; white or non-white – to recognize that seeking self-affirmation by looking at another (by objectifying a human being in order to confirm one's own subjectivity, one's own individuality, one's own social authority) is *always* an ethically flawed, dehumanizing activity. Phelan's "unmarked" feminist performer aims first to undo a viewer's expectations of what her appearance means, and second to confront that viewer with the potential consequences, for her and others, of those expectations. Meanwhile, the scholar of the "unmarked" looks out for such performances of active vanishing, celebrates them, explicates them and encourages more of them.

Gestic feminist criticism: Elin Diamond

Working with Marxist theories of cultural materialism rather than the theories of Freud and Lacan (though nevertheless following Mulvey as an essential predecessor), Elin Diamond takes a slightly different approach to countering the gaze. Inspired by the writings of Bertolt Brecht, she imagines what she calls a "gestic" feminist criticism: a practice where feminist performers do not simply reflect the male gaze but refract it, return it with a difference, and thereby even "dismant[le]" it (*Unmaking Mimesis* 44). In her landmark essay "Brechtian Theory/Feminist Theory," reprinted in *Unmaking Mimesis* in 1997 Diamond argues that "classical mimesis" (49) encourages audience members to adopt an overly simplistic form of seeing, one that leaves us ill equipped to recognize or examine the contradictions working within a play's plot or within its characters.

(Classical mimesis refers to a mode of theatrical imitation in which a "real world" is presented on stage, complete with characters who can often seem fixed into culturally and ideologically determined positions.) Brecht responded to the subtle oppressions of "classical mimesis" by creating a "dialectical" dramaturgy, in which linear plots give way to episodes, and actors play characters as separate from themselves, as figures whose social circumstances warrant discussion and debate. Using this dramaturgy as a model for feminist theatre theory, Diamond argues for a practice of staging women's experiences that may allow the contradictions shaping those experiences to become visible. In a "gestic feminist" dramaturgy, the moments that reveal such contradictions are heightened and foregrounded rather than glossed over; the female characters who bear such contradictions do not turn away in shame but revel in them, looking back at the auditorium with an invitation to spectators to pay attention to the narrative's hidden feminist stories.

Phelan's "*active* vanishing" and Diamond's strategy for using Brechtian tactics to meet the gaze head-on are two sides of the same coin. Each theorizes the "payoff," for female characters, of a refusal to appear on stage *as scripted by our patriarchal culture*; each explores the value, for spectators in the stalls, of refusing to take the stage image and its promises of pleasurable identification on faith. I'll now explore how each of these models might work for the feminist spectator "as critic" in a short discussion of Young Jean Lee's *Untitled Feminist Show* (2012).

Case study 1: *Untitled Feminist Show*, Young Jean Lee's Theater Company (2012)

Young Jean Lee is one of New York's, and America's, most important contemporary playwrights; her feminist, anti-racist work turns assumptions about people of colour, women and LGBTQ subjects hilariously and pointedly on their heads. According to her theatre company's website, in their 2012 work, *Untitled Feminist Show* (*UFS*), "six charismatic stars of the downtown [New York] theater, dance, cabaret, and burlesque worlds come together to invite the audience on an exhilaratingly irreverent, nearly-wordless celebration of a fluid and limitless sense of identity" ("Untitled Feminist Show"). What this promotional blurb chooses *not* to tell us, however, is that its six "charismatic stars" – in the version I saw, these included Becca Blackwell (who identifies as transgendered), Katy Pyle, Desiree Burch, Lady Rizo, Madison Krekel and Jennifer Rosenblit – perform *Untitled Feminist Show* completely naked.

Female nudity is obviously "the hook" for *UFS*, but my own experience of seeing the show at Toronto's Fleck Dance Theatre in February 2014 was that the nudity is not a gimmick in any way: it is resolutely *not* designed to attract a privileged male "gaze." *UFS* begins with the houselights up; slowly, spectators hear Blackwell, Pyle, Burch, Rizo, Krekel and Rosenblit enter from the back of the auditorium, their rhythmic, deliberately laboured breathing the only sound in the space. The sound is weird, a bit robotic, yet the performers' naked bodies are anything but: as I craned my neck to watch them move towards the stage, I realized that I was both gawking at them and struggling to look away. I wanted to show their bodies respect but did not know how. Finally, I realized that I did not need to stare; instead, I could choose to *bear witness* to the bodies, to their nakedness and vulnerability as well as to their obvious strength. The women's slow, precise, deliberate movements through the auditorium offered me ample time to examine imperfect bellies, rolls of fat, sinewy arms and thighs, wrinkles around breasts and on faces – real women's bodies, undressed and unadorned. Meanwhile, as she passed me, each performer looked right into my eyes. I fought to meet her look, and not to blink.

This introductory sequence was, for me, a call to think about what it is that I do – how I look, what I think about as I look, what I expect from my looking, maybe even what I desire as I look – when I watch women's bodies and stories on stage today, in the early twenty-first century. The women were naked, but I felt it was me that was stripped quite bare. Was my looking OK? Or should I look away? As it raises these simple questions, *UFS* taps directly into Phelan's theory of "active vanishing." The show does not call for its female performers *not* to appear, of course, but as it presents them to us in all their imperfect human flesh, fat, muscle and bone it purposefully removes the thing the male gaze always hopes to see: a beautifully made-up, covered-up woman who almost-but-not-quite reveals herself to consuming eyes. The "chaste" female object of the gaze might offer a glimpse of breast but no more, lest her chastity be questioned; meanwhile, a female body staged for sex (for example, that of a female pornography worker) would never move in such a way as to reveal cellulite or wrinkles. The "male gaze" never sees the female *as body*; the gaze is at its most powerful and dangerous when it *denies* that women are human bodies, entitled to full, inalienable human rights and bodily protections (see Gay 267–79). As Blackwell, Pyle, Burch, Rizo, Krekel and Rosenblit prepare to mount the stage each evening, they firmly demand spectators see their bodies *as human bodies*, hear their lungs and limbs physically working for our benefit.

Remember that feminist resistance to the gaze is both visual and structural; it's a matter of both *what* is presented on stage, lifted up to audience view, and *how* that material is presented, the narrative that shapes its presentation. *UFS* is structured not as a linear narrative about a group of women, but as a feminist cabaret that features a series of vignettes in dance and mime (there is almost no speech in the performance). This episodic structure reveals the show's debts to early music hall theatre and the work of Brecht, but also to feminist performance companies like Split Britches or Hot Peaches, who typically stylize their characters and storylines in order to talk back to gendered stereotypes and render them ridiculous – and often very funny. *UFS*'s several vignettes include a fairy tale in which a "witch" (played by Rizo) comically lures a group of girlish "frenemies" away from one another, Rizo's outlandish, grotesque movements countering the feigned innocence and awkwardness of the women playing the nasty girls. There's also a fun, athletic dance number that choreographs "women's work" such as vacuuming, breast feeding, cooking and other chores to a strong, toe-tappingly catchy beat, and a tender, loving *pas-de-deux* between Katy Pyle and Madison Krekel ironically mapped onto The Crystals' 1962 "He Hit Me (And It Felt Like a Kiss)," a song about domestic violence. Perhaps most notorious is this stand-up comedy-style "bit": Rizo wordlessly approaches the footlights, brings up the houselights, pinpoints individual male audience members (her hands shielding her eyes the better to see – really to see! – us) and mimes several detailed sexual gestures (fisting, rimming, giving head), all the while grinning broadly. The night I attended everyone laughed at this vignette, along with Rizo, but as far as I could tell *nobody* wanted to become the object of her forceful, hungry gaze. Our laughter was pretty awkward, in other words.

Many of *UFS*'s set pieces deliberately dramatize hackneyed feminine stereotypes (loving girlfriends/hateful bitches) or easily dismissed or overlooked "female" issues or problems, like harried mommies (in the "women's work" dance) or the casual street harassment of women (which Rizo's bit brilliantly captures and reverses). In each vignette, however, there is also a full-frontal contradiction on view: the gruelling "women's work" dance number is presented with an air of chirpy, cheerleading athleticism; the loving dance is set to a song about beating up a girlfriend; Rizo's stand-up bit insists on her right to harass her male spectators openly, cruelly and yet also comically, referencing how women who object to sexual harassment on the street are typically told to "get a sense of humour." Further, the performers' bald-faced nudity offers a constant, simple, powerful counterpoint to the otherwise predictable scenarios.

Their profoundly *material* nakedness made me, as a feminist spectator, consistently look *twice* at everything I was watching – once at the (superficially "feminist") story being acted out by the six women, and again at the bombshell of their naked performing bodies, as they danced, heaved, ran, jiggled, repeatedly exposed their genitals, sweated and collapsed in front of me.

This material quality of the naked bodies on stage, combined with the show's episodic structure and its prominent display of contradiction, aligns *UFS* directly with Diamond's prescription for a "gestic" feminist practice. Remember that, for Diamond, gestic feminism examines the social, economic, historical, physical and other conditions that frame a female body on stage and determine what that body is free to do, or not do, within the narrative. In this case, Young Jean Lee's performers cite their social contexts with the content of their vignettes, but they also cite the material reality of their bodies as they foreground those bodies in all of their physical differences from one another. Some are fat; some are thin; some are older; some are younger; some are lithe; some move easily; some do not. (Significantly, given Lee's noted focus on the performance of race in other of her shows, all are white.) No body is "normal" because there is no "normal" female body on the *UFS* stage. All, however, are working bodies: the sheer physical exertion it takes each woman, separately and together, to put on *Untitled Feminist Show* is never hidden from our view. If women aren't supposed to sweat, *especially* while looking beautiful for the camera, Blackwell, Pyle, Burch, Rizo, Krekel and Rosenblit expose the trick of the eye that makes such a cultural expectation possible – and also untenable.

Adapting elements of both "active vanishing" and "gestic feminist" practice, *Untitled Feminist Show* asks the deceptively simple question of what it means to look at a female body, on the street and at the theatre, right now. *UFS* is never polemical; instead, it presents us with six naked female bodies, as though these bodies are the most natural, normal thing in the world (fancy that!), and then it invites us to figure out how to deal with them so that we can all get on with the show.

Being versus acting

The strategies that feminist performance scholars have used to redirect and critique the patriarchal gaze have often been inspired by the work of Bertolt Brecht, a German experimental director and committed follower of the political theories of Karl Marx who was active between 1920 and 1956. But Brecht has been important to feminist performance theory and criticism for another reason as well. Brecht's work resists what he calls "culinary" theatre – which for him means everything from melodramas whose music is purely for entertainment purposes, to conventional bourgeois "living room" plays in which tragic outcomes might be predicted from the beginning – and aims instead to demonstrate dialectical materialism on stage. (Dialectical materialism is closely related to cultural materialism; "dialectical" here means to offer two sides of an argument.) Brecht developed stage techniques to reveal the social and economic circumstances shaping characters' experiences and choices on stage; his goal was to encourage audiences to debate the relationship between circumstances (Hedda Gabler feels trapped in her new house) and choices (Hedda, feeling trapped, tries to control everyone around her), rather than to make moral judgements about both characters and choices (Hedda tries to control everyone because she is a mean, controlling woman). In this way, Brecht's theatre theory imagines spectators as active, engaged and politically aware, and primes them to leave the theatre ready to support positive social change in their own worlds.

Brecht's dramas have not been especially popular among feminist critics (see Solomon's essay on *The Good Person of Szechuan* in *Redressing the Canon* [2001], and my essay on *Mother Courage and her Children* [2003], for two notable exceptions), but his commitment to a socially activist dramaturgy made him of significant interest to feminist scholars in the middle of the 1980s, when Elin Diamond explicitly took up the promise of "epic" theory for feminist performance criticism. In the UK, playwright Caryl Churchill's debt to Brecht's techniques as well as his politics had long been plain in *Cloud 9* (1979), *Vinegar Tom* (1976) and *Light Shining in Buckinghamshire* (1976), among her many important early works, and critics articulated the value of Brecht for feminism in the UK by championing Churchill's collaborative work with the Joint Stock and Monstrous Regiment theatre collectives. Then, on the heels of some of Churchill's most celebrated, pointedly political work at the height of the Margaret Thatcher era (including *Top Girls* and *Serious Money*

[1987]), and just as Diamond, Reinelt, Gay Gibson Cima and others were beginning to look critically at Brecht's politics in the US, a landmark development in gender theory aligned Brechtian strategies firmly to feminist performance theory and practice.

Judith Butler as feminist performance critic

Judith Butler's name is now synonymous with the idea of "gender performativity," which argues that gender (identifying, and being identified publically, as a woman or a man) is not innate, a feature of our human biology, but is reproduced over and over again both on and within our bodies as we rehearse gender codes we and our fellow citizens recognize as "normal" (often without even realizing it). Butler writes, "Gender is the repeated stylization of the body, a set of repeated acts within a highly rigid regulatory frame that congeal over time to produce the *appearance of substance, of a natural sort of being*" (*Gender Trouble* 33, my emphasis). Butler is arguing that we only *seem* to be "naturally" (or, as Brecht would say, inevitably) men or women; really, we *create* our genders anew every time we choose how to act, what to wear, how to present ourselves in public. It's important to realize that Butler is *not* arguing that human beings simply choose to "dress" themselves in gender, like a costume, each day; she emphasizes that the "rigid" codes of permissible gendered behaviour are ingrained in our cultures and learned at both conscious and unconscious levels from an extremely young age. In one of her most celebrated examples from her 1993 book *Bodies That Matter*, the reproduction of appropriate gender behaviour begins before we have any control over it, when the doctor in the delivery room announces over a squalling baby's body: "it's a girl!" or "it's a boy!" As Butler says wryly, nobody in the birth room ever announces: "it's a lesbian!" (232).

The implications of Butler's work on gender performativity have been wide-reaching and formative for social justice advocates; as she argues in *Gender Trouble* (1990) and *Bodies That Matter*, as well as in later, more broadly political books such as *Precarious Life* (2004), "correct" performances of sex and gender, when read alongside those performances a society considers unacceptable or morally wrong, directly determine whose bodies and whose rights we are willing to defend and whose lives we are willing to protect. Butler's writings have also, however, profoundly impacted the development of feminist and queer (LGBTQ) performance theory. Even though she is a cultural philosopher and not a theatre scholar, Butler's work was directly connected to the institutional development of feminist performance theory: one of her most important early essays, "Performative Acts and Gender Constitution: An Essay in Phenomenology and Feminist Theory" (1988), first appeared in *Theatre Journal*, and the essay was subsequently reprinted in Case's *Performing Feminisms*. Butler's appearance in the pages of *TJ* signalled a key theoretical alignment between her work on gender performativity and feminist theories about gender on stage; it also made a very strong case for a specific *kind* of performance practice as "good" for non-normative bodies, and thus as good for feminism.

Butler makes a clear distinction in "Performative Acts and Gender Constitution" between performances of gender at the theatre and performances of gender in public spaces. She argues that the risks of appearing "not normal" in the street are much higher than they are at the theatre, where boys dressed as girls (for example) can be clearly marked as "just [acting]," as performing "something quite distinct from what is real" (527). At this moment in her essay Butler advocates for theatrical performances in which the lines between imagination and reality are *not* clearly drawn – in which what happens on stage can be seen to be trying out new, fairer options for inhabiting our shared social reality. At the same time, though, she expresses an implicit doubt that the theatre can ever be an effective place to subvert "normal" gender practices or categories, given that so much scripted drama relies on the projection of a familiar set of codes onto an acting body that is marked as "normal" and "natural" – or clearly *not* normal or natural – based on its role in the dramatic narrative. (Hedda Gabler and Blanche Dubois are considered powerful, "dramatic" characters precisely because both are written to appear abnormal – not feminine enough, or too feminine – and therefore also "hysterical" [see Diamond, "Realism's Hysteria," in *Unmaking Mimesis*].)

When Butler links mainstream narrative theatre (in which normal opposes abnormal in order to increase dramatic tension) with the mechanisms by which human beings "cite" (that is, perform socially) "normal" gendered behaviour in order to become approved subjects ("proper" men and women), she effectively describes narrative drama as one tool by which gender identities are normalized and rendered binary (man vs woman) in the public sphere. At this point, her theory of gender performativity collides with Brecht's complaints about culinary theatre and the "epic" strategies he proposed for counterbalancing it. This parallel was not lost on the feminist scholars writing in the late 1980s and early 1990s: they realized that, if read together, Butler's and Brecht's theories could offer feminist performance a model for an engaged and ethical theatre practice in which sex and gender codes could be actively and openly contested (and even reimagined) on stage. In theory, any dramatic genre, matched to an appropriately critical form of acting and directorial practice, might accomplish this kind of politically activist resistance to ingrained sex and gender norms; for example, Brecht's own work often paired realist narratives *within* scenes with a compare-and-contrast, episodic approach to a play's larger structure. In practice, however, much feminist performance scholarship took Butler's cue and turned vocally away from stage realism – the epitome of dramatic, narrative theatre – in order to champion non-realist theatrical practices and avant-garde performance art makers who were already engaging playfully with cultural assumptions about sex and gender. Inspired by Butler and modelled on Brecht, feminist performance theory aligned itself openly with self-reflexive "acting" rather than apparent "being" on stage – with practices that sought to stage gender *as a performance* that might be staged differently, rather than with practices that encouraged actors to live a gendered role with the forceful commitment of a Stanislavskian or "Method" actor.

This alignment was an ethical and a political choice; it shaped the plays and productions feminist performance critics chose to explore, debate and celebrate until the early 2000s.

Feminist theory, non-realist practice

The feminist resistance to stage realism took two separate forms, though these are sometimes not clearly distinguished. The first was a resistance to realist *drama*: the well-made, three- or four-act play that all too often features a challenging female character at its core, a woman whose resistance to the feminine propriety dictated by her society makes her troublesome. Ibsen's Hedda, Strindberg's Miss Julie, Pinero's Mrs Tanqueray, Shaw's Mrs Warren, Williams's Laura or Blanche: all exemplify the ways in which the early modernist "problem" play was above all about "problem" women, the difficulties they create for those around them, and the pleasures they afford in finally being figured out, reprimanded or cured. In the US context, the feminist resistance to realist dramaturgy was particularly pronounced given Broadway's dominance by powerful male dramatists such as Arthur Miller or Sam Shepard, whose concerns with masculinity often meant a tight focus on men's issues at the expense of complex women characters. A number of feminists have written acclaimed realist works for Broadway, of course, including Wendy Wasserstein (*The Heidi Chronicles* [1988], which won the Pulitzer Prize) and Paula Vogel (*How I Learned to Drive* [1997]), and more recently African American playwright Lynn Nottage has achieved broad acclaim as a realist committed to writing about black women's experiences (*Crumbs From the Table of Joy* [1995], *Intimate Apparel* [2003], *Ruined* [2007–8]). Nevertheless, the powerful mutual influence and support shared by experimental feminist artists and feminist performance academics meant that more "mainstream" feminist work was not often written about as significant until the end of the 1990s. The economic climate governing the development of new plays within the largely unsubsidized mainstream US repertory system is also partly to blame for academic resistance to its output: the need to fill theatres means that tidy narrative dramas featuring meaty, emotional roles – including problem women – are especially prized by this system, whether those roles are written by women or (more often) by men.

The UK and Canadian contexts offer a somewhat different perspective on stage realism's relationship to feminism. In the UK, realist drama has, since the mid-twentieth century, been associated with socialist realism (that is, with Brecht and Karl Marx) and with the progressive politics espoused at London's Royal Court Theatre. This has meant that feminist critiques of realist plays by both men and women have rarely extended to a wholesale rejection of the form. Many notable British feminist dramas of the middle and later twentieth century, from Shelagh Delaney's *A Taste of Honey* (1958) to Sarah Daniels's *Masterpieces* (1983) to Gurpreet Kaur Bhatti's *Behzti (Dishonour)* (2004), use conventional stage realism in order to voice both feminist and anti-racist positions, and Elaine Aston has recently explored how stage realism empowers new writing by ethnic minority artists within the British theatre's circle of influence ("Room for Realism").

In Canada, the nationalist movement in the theatre during the 1960s and 1970s encouraged both male and female playwrights to fiddle with form and genre, adopting as well as subverting realist practices in order to express anti-colonial and Indigenous as well as feminist and LGBTQ perspectives. Historically significant Canadian feminist playwrights such as Judith Thompson (*White Biting Dog* [1984], *Lion in the Streets* [1990]) and Sharon Pollock (*Blood Relations* [1980], *Doc* [1984]), as well as newcomers like Tara Beagan (*Dreary and Izzy* [2005], *Miss Julie: Sheh'mah* [2008]), Djanet Sears (*Afrika Solo* [1987], *Harlem Duet* [1997]) and Marjorie Chan (*China Doll* [2004], *A Nanking Winter* [2008]) all treat stage realism as a tool rather than as an orthodoxy, using it as a way to strengthen national and community storytelling while also deconstructing realist forms from within.

Alongside, and perhaps louder than, its resistance to realist dramaturgy has been feminist performance theory and criticism's opposition to the technical practices of naturalist acting, attributable to Konstantin Stanislavsky and Lee Strasberg (creators of "The System" and "The Method," respectively). Although Stanislavsky's commitment to a realist aesthetic was only partial (see Carnicke 107–23, esp. 120–1), and although Strasberg's version of Stanislavsky's "System" departs significantly from Stanislavsky's teachings (see Carnicke 1–10 and Malague 16–21), Stanislavsky's influence over actor training in the performance mainstream has been considerable in both the UK and North America. Throughout the 1980s and 1990s, feminist performance scholars argued that emotional realist acting practices are politically unhelpful because emotional realism "laminates body to character" (Diamond, *Unmaking Mimesis* 52), thereby making the different social, political and economic frameworks governing both actors' and characters' gendered behaviours invisible underneath the smooth sheen of "truth" projected by the script. Unlike the Brechtian model, in which actors step visibly in and out of character on stage the better to show audiences the different options available to all of us within the play's reality, the emotional realist model insists above all that actors disappear behind or into their characters while those characters make a "believable" journey from beginning to end of a play. Often, as feminist scholars and practitioners have noted, that journey's dramatic tension arises at the expense of female characters' needs, aspirations and overall well-being. A difficult woman's journey is likely to end either in heartbreak for her or in a too-neat happy ending, or else it risks being criticized as not believable – as though real-world believability were somehow easily captured by the two-plus hours of a scripted fiction in which women are always a problem, and a solution is always close at hand.

Reconsidering realism

The feminist resistance to both realist dramaturgy and emotional realist performance practice became itself a kind of "normal" through the end of the twentieth century. It was fuelled by provocative, invigorating essays such as Diamond's "Brechtian Theory/Feminist Theory" and Reinelt's "Beyond Brecht: Britain's New Feminist Drama," and further inspired by a brace of exceptional readings of outstanding new feminist performance art at the WOW Café, where scholars and artists mixed freely and traded ideas as well as pleasures. (See Davy, *Lady Dicks and Lesbian Brothers*, for a superb historical reading of the influence of the WOW Café.) Within this moving, often joyous context, budding scholars like me could not easily imagine a different model for a truly politically engaged feminist practice. And yet, even as we revelled in Brechtian-feminist antics, some of the very best feminist theatre criticism was exploring realist dramaturgy in serious depth, mining it for its feminist possibilities.

In *Performing Women: Female Characters, Male Playwrights, and the Modern Stage* (1993), Gay Gibson Cima engages with plays by Ibsen, Strindberg, Beckett, Pinter, Shepard and Brecht in order to examine the "actual performance conditions and conventions" that governed the creation of women characters by female actors working in collaboration with these male playwrights (2). Cima's careful archival research about what *actually* happens when men and women work together to put realist (among other styles of) plays on stage makes her book a lively and essential addition to the feminist canon of writings on stage realism. As Cima discovers in the work of American feminist actor and playwright Elizabeth Robins, who brought Ibsen's Hedda to the London stage, and in the work of the several women who were instrumental in the production of Brecht's plays: "Successful feminist actors ... highlight competing codes, reminding audiences that their bodies cannot be subsumed into any given style" (7).

Not long after Cima's book appeared, Elin Diamond published *Unmaking Mimesis* (1997), the culmination of her important late 1980s work and the text that marks her as one of the most important feminist theatre theorists of the twentieth century. In this book, which includes an expanded version of "Brechtian Theory/Feminist Theory" alongside readings of works by Ibsen, Churchill, Aphra Behn, Adrienne Kennedy, Robbie McCauley and WOW Café artists Peggy Shaw and Deb Margolin, Diamond does not position feminist performance *against* stage realism as much as she argues that realist dramaturgy and stage practices themselves embed a series of internal contradictions that feminist performance can and should exploit. In her first chapter, "Realism's Hysteria," Diamond reads Ibsen's *Hedda Gabler* through the work of actress Elizabeth Robins (also discussed by Cima). Diamond examines the minute ways in which Robins, like a forensic pathologist, looked for clues of Hedda's clinical hysteria in Ibsen's text, and then sought intricate ways to portray her behaviour accurately on stage. She also, however, notes how Robins's performance of Hedda always exceeded the clues she offered audiences about the character's welfare, suggesting someone who was not simply ill but who was actively made sick by a society that tried to wedge her into the role of wealthy bourgeois housewife and mother. In this way, Diamond argues, realist plays can indeed – with care – historicize and critique the social circumstances of the "difficult" women that feature so prominently in their plotlines.

Diamond has a name for the "excess" that escapes characters like Hedda in performance: realism's hysteria. Note that Diamond does not claim that all realist female characters are hysterics; she argues, instead, that all realist dramaturgy subtly embeds competing social contexts, and thus that all realist plays can be staged in a way that demonstrates their internal contradictions, rather than smoothing them over to create internal consistency and "believable" character journeys. "Realism's Hysteria" implies that realist dramaturgy is not so different from Brechtian dramaturgy after all; what matters is the *way* feminists explore and prepare that material for a critically evocative staging of sex and gender issues. Such a staging might, for example, focus attention not on Hedda's apparent descent into madness in the final act, but rather on the complexities of Hedda's reactions throughout the play as she comes fully to realize Tesman's and Lovborg's expectations of her in her new role as a decorative housewife. Read through such a prism, her choice to commit suicide makes material (social, political), rather than pathological, sense.

Diamond's return to realist dramaturgy with a critical feminist eye was a welcome development in the late 1990s and early 2000s, when feminist performance scholars were beginning to rethink the ways in which certain kinds of work had been inadvertently (or, sometimes, deliberately) excluded from view by the discipline's political resistance to realism. Some of the most provocative of these rethinkings came from younger scholars raised on the essential texts of 1980s feminist performance theory. In 2007, Roberta Barker published *Early Modern Tragedy, Gender and Performance, 1984–2000: The Destined Livery*, which explored (among other topics) the feminist potential of realist acting techniques in mainstream British performances of Shakespeare and his contemporaries. Given that large theatre organizations such as the Royal Shakespeare Company (RSC) are unlikely to abandon the financial draws of realism anytime soon, Barker, like Cima and Diamond before her, carefully parses the strategies performers and directors have employed to convey complex, multifaceted realities in productions at major theatre venues that typically demand believable, journey-focused acting. In her reading of the 1995 Cheek by Jowl production of John Webster's *The Duchess of Malfi* (c. 1613), for example, Barker examines Anastasia Hille's aristocratic, hyper-feminine Duchess and George Anton's class-bound Bosola as inextricably linked, drawing attention to the intersections of gender and social constraints in the making of each of their performances of "self" (see Barker 55–82). For Barker's feminist spectator, Hille's Duchess is not simply too feminine, nor simply overly ambitious, nor simply doomed for trying to be both; rather, she inhabits several competing subject positions uneasily and simultaneously, actively navigating the contradictions that shape her status as *both* a woman *and* a ruler at a time and in a place that can barely fathom a female head of state.

Feminist realism officially entered the critical mainstream in a 2008 special issue of *Theatre Journal* called "Feminism and Theatre, Redux." It featured two articles, by Dorothy Chansky and Jill Dolan, that looked afresh at the work of popular feminist writers such as Betty Friedan (*The Feminine Mystique*, [1963]) and Wendy Wasserstein.

Dolan and Chansky argued forcefully that the dismissal of popular feminist artists by academics working in performance criticism was no longer tenable after 9/11, the election of George W. Bush, and the broad feminist backlash that accompanied these events in the US. Dolan's essay focuses on the political urgency of remembering Broadway feminism in a historical moment that was (and perhaps still is) fundamentally disinterested in theoretical sophistication. "In 2008, not enough feminist performance work is visible or taken seriously for scholars to make the fine distinctions [between mainstream and avant-garde] that once seemed necessary," she argues, and "after eight years of the Bush administration and the taste it has left of the most chilling sorts of ideological conservatism, I believe that progressive feminists can no longer afford to disparage one another's work or split critical hairs about which forms, contexts, and contents do more radically activist work" (435). Chansky takes a less directly political position than Dolan, but one that is arguably more sympathetic to the inherent feminist value of the mainstream theatre she invokes:

> Feminist theatre today is a plural; indeed ... it has been a plural almost since its inception, although the critical concerns of the 1980s and 1990s obscured the importance of the work of feminists like Wasserstein and even Jane Chambers and Eve Ensler [author of *The Vagina Monologues,* 1996]. Feminist theatre writ large encompasses postmodern, theoretically inflected work that

> may or may not even be primarily concerned
> with a play text and a linear argument; it also
> embraces realism that appeals to those uninter-
> ested in high theory. (362)

In these thoughtful, self-reflective essays, Chansky and
Dolan admirably revisit feminist performance theory's earlier commitments to a less populist academic feminism,
demonstrating the discipline's willingness to critique itself
and look anew at old orthodoxies. They also open the door
for other scholars to take more seriously work produced for
a popular audience (see, for example, *A Good Night Out For
The Girls*, edited by Elaine Aston and Geraldine Harris),
work invested in conventional generic forms such as stage
realism, and work interested in exploring the labour of
"being," rather than self-consciously "acting," the part of the
woman on stage.

Case study 2: *A Doll's House*, dir. Carrie Cracknell (2012)

London's Young Vic theatre is known for bridging the gap
between "intellectual" and "popular" performance. It pro-
grams work that is at once visually spectacular and politically
challenging, appealing to an audience of secondary school
and university students of varying income levels, scholars,
London theatre folk and "small-l" liberal, typically middle-
class subscribers. Over the last few years the Young Vic has
made a notable commitment to producing fresh translations
of classic realist plays, particularly by Anton Chekhov and

Henrik Ibsen; this trend took wing in 2012 with director Carrie Cracknell and playwright Simon Stephens's version of *A Doll's House* by Ibsen, starring Hattie Morahan in a career-making turn as the play's main character, Nora. Nora begins Ibsen's play as a charming yet manipulative bourgeois wife and mother, striving to make ends meet while her husband Torvald knows little of the household's precarious financial situation; she ends by walking out on Torvald after realizing that she has been no genuine partner in their marriage, and is not capable of being a mother to her children because she is not yet a person to herself. Slamming the door of the flat behind her, Nora makes a commitment to freeing herself from her assigned gender role, to educating herself and to becoming the woman Torvald's household would never freely allow to emerge. Enormously controversial in its first productions in the late nineteenth century, *A Doll's House* is now, after more than a century of feminist activism in the political mainstream, considered canonical, a quintessentially popular piece of feminist realist theatre. Perhaps unsurprisingly then, Cracknell's conventional-looking period production and strong cast won rave reviews and numerous awards from a wide range of critics before transferring first to London's West End and then to Broadway. And yet, there is much more to this production than first meets the eye.

Buzzing from the moment she enters the flat in Act One, her hands fluttering anxiously and her voice ramped up to a level of intensity that seems almost unsustainable, Morahan's Nora reads to a feminist spectator like a woman working very hard indeed to keep all of the pieces of her life together. Her Nora endures daily the difficult physical and emotional labour of managing a household and its scarce monetary resources, its servants and visitors, her children's expectations of their fun-loving mom, and her husband's expectations of his slightly flighty, attractively naïve wife, all the while trying to find a few moments simply to stop and catch her breath, perhaps eat a sweet or two. Her hands fly to her mouth and forehead, her lips twitch between requisite glowing smile and the concern that lies beneath her veneer of constant joy: in these simple gestures Morahan signals that Nora understands in her body, at the level of her motor memory, that her job as Torvald Helmer's songbird-wife is both to act in and to direct the performance of *his* pleasure, comfort and ease.

Morahan's performance in Cracknell's production reminds me strongly of her earlier work under the pre-eminent naturalist director Katie Mitchell, including as the teenage Iphigenia in *Iphigenia at Aulis* (2004) and as the young actress Nina in Chekhov's *The Seagull* (2006), on which Cracknell also worked. During this period, Mitchell was experimenting with a combination of Russian acting theory influenced by Stanislavsky and Lev Dodin, and cognitive science research on ways physically to transmit sensations of anxiety and dread between actors and audience members (see Shevtsova). In a personal interview in July 2014 Morahan confirmed to me that her work on Nora was significantly influenced by the time she spent with Mitchell, and particularly by Mitchell's commitment to the standard emotional realist techniques of extensive improvisation and the building of complete character histories. The impression Morahan creates with her harried Nora, her voice and mannerisms utterly composed and yet always just moments from breaking, startled me on all three occasions I saw the show live in exactly the way Mitchell might have wished: my heartbeat increased in line with Nora's amplified tension, heightening my physiological as well as my emotional engagement with her actions on stage. The impression Nora left on my body was also a *political* one, however, because Morahan works to physicalize Nora's anxiety and extreme exhaustion precisely in order to convey a historicized, socially and economically informed "truth" about Nora's "being" in Ibsen's play. Her physically and emotionally taxing performance demonstrates that the apparent pleasures of Nora's seemingly charmed life, including her dancing and tricks and constant smiles for the wallet-clutching Torvald, are all *work*: the work of a performance labourer (someone who plays a role for money) in what we might call the early bourgeois "creative economy."

Today, we understand the "creative economy" (an insidious feature of neoliberal capitalism, which I discuss in the opening section of this book) as one in which everyone from advertising professionals to teachers to retail staff are invited to view themselves as creative performers in jobs that have been relabelled as somehow artistic, as more "fun" than "work." With its characteristic focus on "flexible scheduling" and "entrepreneurial freedom" the creative economy *sounds* enormously appealing, but in reality a lot of freshly labelled "creative" jobs are emotionally draining, poorly compensated and offer almost no job security. (Imagine for a moment the hidden offstage life of the last bubbly waiter who served you at a popular chain restaurant, and you'll see what I mean.) Morahan's performance in Cracknell's production offers audiences a feminist, historical view of the creative economy familiar to us today: her performance suggests that housewives like Nora have been "creative" workers for as long as they have been expected both to keep and to "decorate" their husbands' homes. In the brief moments when she is alone in the first act the contrast between Nora "on" and Nora "off" is plainly marked by Morahan's actions: she slows down for the briefest of moments, allows her face to fall gently, allows herself to come to rest. This pivot reads as a deliberate pause on stage, making starkly apparent how very hard the work of "being Nora" is – both for Nora and for Hattie Morahan.

Significantly, Morahan is the only performer in Cracknell's production who works at this high a pitch; all of the other performances read as moderate in comparison. For a feminist spectator this contrast in performance styles creates a valuable tension, an "excess" that maps well onto what Diamond calls realism's hysteria. Morahan styles Nora as a woman riddled with contradictions: she is a wife who has never known what to do, if not look pretty; a woman who must take in sewing to pay her secret debts but must never show the ugliness of physical labour to her sensitive husband or his friends; a woman who must play the role of mommy to her children because she has never known a mother, nor what it means to be a mother. Morahan's acting choices, all of them realist in technique, bring these contradictions into focus as her Nora struggles to fit the disparate parts of herself together into an attractive, "believable," middle-class package, a story other people are happy to hear. The fact that she must fight this fight, that she cannot just naturally inhabit the roles her job requires her to play every day, *is Nora's reality* – as well as the play's open secret – in this production. Morahan and Cracknell create a feminist realist portrait of a woman who can never simply "be" the woman everyone expects her to be; her reality is apparent to audiences from start to finish as an obligatory, highly skilled, enormously onerous performance of femininity in a historical moment not so very far removed from our own. (To accompany this production Cracknell made a short film called *Nora*, also starring Morahan. Easily accessible online at www.the-guardian.com and on YouTube, it transplants the character into a middle class London suburb in 2012.)

In the play's famous final scene, which Nora brings to a close as she walks out the door, the meticulousness of Morahan's performance cracks open. Nora's coming to know consciously over the course of the play what her body has perhaps always known – that this is no life; that her husband barely regards her as human – abruptly alters Morahan's physical and emotional bearing. Now her Nora is stunned, quiet, no longer fluttering; then she is reasoning, coming to terms logically with her unfolding understanding of how useless her relationship with Torvald and the children has truly been. Then she is sobbing, shouting,

hitting Torvald so forcefully that I am utterly riveted, daz-
zled, crushed, smiling on the verge of tears. Morahan's
performance in these final moments shifts uncomfortably
beyond "emotional realism" as acting practice and into the
"real" of human emotion, of the human brain and body
fully overwhelmed by what it is going through in this very
moment, right here in front of us. Pressing towards Nora's
climactic exit, Morahan approaches more closely than ever
Diamond's version of realism's hysteria. Nora is not sick,
not herself "hysterical," despite Torvald's insistence to the
contrary in this scene. She is both a performer (Morahan)
and a character (Nora) engaged in battering, in real time
here with us all, the walls that trap her in a limiting version
of who she might yet become.

Hope and loss

The last two sections of *Theatre & Feminism* have focused
on two important historical dimensions of feminist performance theory and criticism, both of which continue to influence contemporary feminist scholars and artists. In this last
main section of the book I'd like to turn towards the present, and to the question of where feminist scholars and artists interested in theatre and performance are focusing their
attentions right now.

Feminist performance theory in the wake of terror

Our feminist present is indelibly marked by the large-scale
atrocities that have wreaked havoc for human rights across
the globe over the last two decades, including the Gulf War

of 1990–1, the Iraq War of 2003–11, the Bosnian War of 1992–5, the genocide against the Tutsi people in Rwanda in April 1994, the terrorist insurgency perpetrated by Boko Haram in Nigeria (2009–), and the current war in Syria (2011–) and in the broader Middle East against ISIS. These are just a representative handful of recent international conflicts that have seen rape and other forms of violence against women mobilized as a weapon of war (especially in the Balkans, Rwanda and Nigeria), and intimate sexual practices weaponized by the US military (at Abu Ghraib prison, among many other locations). The former subject has been taken up by feminist playwrights such as Colleen Wagner in Canada (*The Monument*, 1995) and Lynn Nottage in the US (*Ruined*, 2007–8), while the latter features in Judith Thompson's *Palace of the End* (2005) and is the focus of Latina-American artist and scholar Coco Fusco's *A Field Guide for Female Interrogators* (2008), part of her extensive *Operation Atropos* performance project (for which Fusco and female colleagues underwent military training in prisoner interrogation tactics). Collectively, this work represents the increasingly international focus of feminist theatre and performance originating in English-speaking nations, as Anglophone artists try to come to terms with the urgent needs of girls and women in politically unstable or extremely socially conservative nations, as well as with the complicity of many of their home nations in those women's continued struggle for safety and security.

A similarly outward focus has taken root among feminist performance theorists, many of whom are working to bring much-needed attention to feminist playwrights and performers in at-risk states while also extending their scholarly collaborations to include both artists and academics from non-English-speaking nations. Exactly this kind of transnational, collaborative work makes up the recent collections *Feminist Futures? Theatre, Performance, Theory*, edited by Elaine Aston and Geraldine Harris (2006), *Staging International Feminisms*, edited by Aston and Sue-Ellen Case (2007), and *Contemporary Women Playwrights: Into the Twenty-First Century*, edited by Penny Farfan and Lesley Ferris (2014). *Staging International Feminisms* emerged from the Feminist Research Working Group at the International Federation for Theatre Research, which has long been at the vanguard of the push to recognize feminist theatre and performance as necessarily international in scope, multilingual, multiracial and multidisciplinary. Case, Aston, Jill Dolan, Elin Diamond, Janelle Reinelt and other pioneering feminist performance theorists remain part of the group, alongside numerous next-generation scholars, as well as important established scholars from beyond the Anglosphere, including Fawzia Afzal-Khan, Tiina Rosenberg, and Bishnupriya Paul-Dutt.

While many Anglophone feminist scholars are now looking beyond the UK and the US, two major events that took place at the beginning of this century in the United States nevertheless had a profound impact on the direction feminist performance theory and criticism has taken over the last 15 years. These events were the election of George W. Bush as US president in November 2000 (his tenure would last until 2008), and the large-scale suicide attacks on New York

City and the Pentagon in Washington, DC on 11 September 2001. Together, they ushered in a new era of heightened security and racial panic in America, one marked by a renewed and fervent nationalism, by an anxiety about the beliefs and intentions of Arab and Muslim men and women, as well as by an increased sympathy for social conservatism, a branch of conservative ideology interested in advocating for social, gender and sexual norms.

In the wake of these events and the political turmoil they provoked, theatre scholars began asking questions about the place of theatre and performance in a world increasingly shaped by the US-authored "War on Terror"; one of the results was a special issue of *Theatre Journal* focused on theatre and tragedy, produced under the editorship of the queer Latino scholar David Román. As part of the issue, a number of feminist scholars and scholars with feminist sympathies drawn from across the Americas – including Diamond, Dolan and Case, as well as Jill Lane, José Esteban Muñoz, Alicia Arrízon and Jennifer DeVere Brody – contributed to "A Forum on Theater and Tragedy: A Response to September 11, 2001." As a group, the forum authors spoke to the potential repercussions of the attacks on New York and Washington for everyone concerned about women's rights, LGBTQ rights, the rights of racial and cultural minorities, and democratic freedom more broadly, both on and off the stage, in America and everywhere the "War on Terror" was being felt.

A quite personal reflection on the rights and freedoms of women and minorities in the wake of 11 September 2001 appears in Sharon P. Holland's contribution to the Forum. Holland tells the story of how she learned about the attacks while on a cottage holiday in rural Wisconsin with her female partner. Craving contact with fellow citizens after being immersed in the news for hours on end, she and her partner headed for a restaurant in the nearest town. Holland describes feeling "palpable" hostility from their server and fellow diners as soon as they walked in (118). On this day, marked by an event for which threatening "others" was being endlessly blamed on TV and online, they felt, Holland explains, plainly not welcome, not a part of the community of fellow citizens gathered around the restaurant's television. Uncomfortable, they briefly considered leaving, but then chose to stay and eat their dinner. Of this decision, she writes:

> Perhaps it was foolish to walk into a small town watering hole and not expect "trouble" on September 11th. But to remain at home ... would have meant that the ordinary rhythm of my life – the coming and the going – would heretofore be circumscribed by *what if*. Instead, if I allow *was is* to contour my days, I can remember a way of being in the world that makes the quotidian look like less of a battlefield and more of an opportunity. (119)

For Holland, this difficult personal experience becomes a fruitful site for feminist critique, as well as for hopeful theorizing. In her conception, "what if" represents a failure to engage critically with the most difficult moments in our shared pasts, while "was is" represents the (very feminist) notion that the past and the present are never separate. If, Holland suggests, the events of the past shape our present world for better and for worse, it is ultimately up to each one of us to think carefully, critically, and with compassion about what our shared histories signify, and about how we would like them to impact our collective present and shape our shared future.

Feminist feelings at the theatre: Jill Dolan and Elaine Aston

The interplay between loss (part of a traumatic, shared past that lives on in our present world) and hope (for a better and fairer collective future) animating Holland's Forum contribution became an important trend in feminist performance scholarship in the years after 2001, and it animates in particular the influential late work of pioneering theorist Jill Dolan. Shortly after the election of George W. Bush to the White House in 2000, and while she was the director of the "Performance as a Public Practice" postgraduate stream at the University of Texas, Austin, Dolan began work on the project that would become *Utopia in Performance: Finding Hope at the Theater* (2005). *Utopia in Performance* represents a shift in Dolan's scholarship away from work that is firmly entrenched in her identity as a feminist and lesbian, and towards a practice of what she calls (in line with other millennial scholars) "a new, more radical humanism" (2). This practice is feminist in its spirit, its outlook and its commitment to equal human rights for all subjects, but it also opens its arms wide to include a variety of subjects, including men from LGBTQ and other minority communities.

Dolan's readings throughout the book look for what she calls "utopian performatives" at the theatre; these are "small but profound moments in which performance calls the attention of the audience in a way that lifts everyone slightly above the present" (5) and towards a consideration of "what *if*" (as opposed to "what should be") (13). While it uses different terminology to make its case, Dolan's "what if" closely parallels Holland's "was is." The question of "what if?" for Dolan is always a political one, always an *activist* one, and it is always directed at audiences as groups of citizens who share the ongoing project of living in, creating, and sustaining genuine democracy in the face of a dispersed global terror movement on one hand, and, on the other, an increasingly entrenched turn towards neoliberalism and corporate rights as a governance model across the globe (11). In order to capture its strong political and economic dimensions, Dolan directly aligns her utopian performative to Brecht's idea of "gestus," so important to Diamond's and Reinelt's re-imaginings of his theory for feminist performance in the 1980s. Defining *gestus* as "action[s] in performance that crystallize social relations and offer them to spectators for critical contemplation" (7), Dolan also explains, however, that her utopian performative departs from this central Brechtian concept in an important way. While Brecht's *gestus* is designed to disrupt spectators' emotional attachment to events on stage and invite them instead to think seriously about those events (and about our attachments to them), Dolan's utopian performative regards our emotional attachments to events and characters on stage as part of its critical arsenal. She writes:

> [U]topian performatives are the received moment of gestus, when those well-delineated, moving pictures of social relations become not only intellectually clear but *felt* and *lived* by spectators as well as actors. (7, my emphasis)

In this way, utopian performatives function, for Dolan, as "affective rehearsals for revolution" (7) in a broadly-defined feminist *and* humanist public sphere animated by an emotional relationship between those who create for and act on the stage, and those who attend performance with open hearts and minds.

Utopia in Performance has made a significant impression upon a wide range of theatre and performance scholarship over the past decade, but it has also been critiqued for what some readers view as a too-sentimental attachment to "feel good" moments at the theatre. Erring on the side of hope, Dolan's book leaves work to be done by fellow feminist scholars on the often-overlooked impact of social, economic and political *losses* sustained by women as part of the socially conservative backlash that followed the events of 2000 and 2001. (I discuss some of these losses in the opening section of this book.) In 2011, Elaine Aston synthesized a number of these concerns in an important stock-taking essay called "Feeling the Loss of Feminism: Sarah Kane's *Blasted* and an Experiential Genealogy of Contemporary Women's Playwriting."

In "Feeling the Loss of Feminism," Aston places the growing interest in affect and emotion in theatre and performance theory over the previous decade into conversation with Angela McRobbie's concerns about the ways in which pervasive neoliberal politics have gutted feminism as a movement and damaged its social influence. For Aston, the disappearance of feminism as a genuine political choice for many women over the course of the 1990s and 2000s is directly related to a feeling, an "impression" that feminism is "redundant and over" (577). (In using the term "impression" in this way Aston follows the cultural theorist Sarah Ahmed, for whom the word represents a psychological as well as a physical sensation, the feeling of being literally *impressed upon* by an experience [576].) For Aston, the paradigm I sketched out at the beginning of this book – in which women living in democratic, post-industrialized nations today find themselves uneasy about the label "feminist" – is first and foremost a *felt* experience. It is a sensation (rather than a firm understanding or a clear knowledge) that feminism's work is "over," that women have already "won," and that feminism therefore cannot capture a contemporary woman's experience of being in the world today. Neoliberal culture relentlessly privileges how each of us feels, using social media and soft political messaging to create blasts of good feeling despite the ugly reality of daily news cycles, and despite the less than ideal material conditions in which many of us objectively live our lives. In this context, Aston argues, feminism has come to be associated with negative and inauthentic feelings, and those feelings have a lot of power over us.

In response to this pervasive sensation that feminism is no longer relevant, Aston argues that contemporary British playwrights Sarah Kane (d. 1999) and debbie tucker green create work that stages the "loss of feminism" as something we may in turn *feel at the theatre*, in order to explore critically the consequences of that loss for contemporary culture. Importantly, the playwrights Aston discusses do not always adopt a feminist position directly. Rather, like Jessica Pabón, whose work on Chilean graffiti artists I discussed earlier in this book, Aston excavates Kane's and tucker green's writing in order better to understand how their choice to *disavow* an explicit feminist position may result in performances that generate a deeply felt response to what it means *not* to have a feminist position to turn to in order to make sense of the brutal violence or the shocking misogyny around us.

Aston's discussion of Sarah Kane's *Blasted* (1995) is the major case study shaping "Feeling the Loss of Feminism," and it constitutes an important reclaiming of Kane for feminist performance scholarship. Kane rose to prominence as a representative of "the laddish culture of in-yer-face theatre" in the 1990s (580), but *Blasted* is, Aston notes, first and foremost "a domestic rape story" (580) that quickly and literally blows up into total war, modelled in part on the Bosnian conflict, in which the integrity of no human body is safe. Kane uses a series of shock-and-awe tactics to

force audiences to experience the events of the play viscerally, a choice that triggered a notorious backlash, primarily from male theatre critics, after *Blasted*'s premier at the
Royal Court Theatre Upstairs in 1995 (see Saunders). Aston
argues that Kane assaults our typically protected and safely
distanced spectating bodies with "viscerally and emotionally charged connections" that link "the damaging and dehumanizing consequences of sexual violence and epic warfare"
together in a way that invites us to understand the rape of
a woman in a hotel room in Leeds as part of a fundamen-
tal crisis in British culture, indeed in "Western" culture, as
a whole (Aston, "Feeling the Loss" 578). *Blasted* asks that
we witness a crisis moment in which large-scale human
destruction is literally born from the sexual assault of a
woman – a profoundly feminist gesture – even if we have,
and if the play offers us, no intellectual or ideological tools
to make sense of that connection in the immediate moment
of our watching.

Sarah Kane did not identity as a feminist playwright or
even as a "woman writer" (576) in her lifetime, but she did
identify as someone whose work sought to challenge the
casual disregard for savage injustice against both women and
minority subjects that has become the hallmark of the post-
Thatcher era in Britain. For Aston, it is these two facts –
Kane's deep commitment to what must be recognized as
feminist *action* alongside her blatant, heartfelt refusal of a
feminist *identity* – that make her representative of a new
generation of artists for whom feminism lies primarily in
doing rather than being, and for whom that doing is both

politically urgent but also marked by a profound loss of collective feeling. Comparing Kane's outright refusal of feminist attachment with Caryl Churchill's cautious but much firmer commitment to the term in a 1977 interview (576), Aston writes:

> [Kane's] theatre figures the generational feminist shift from Churchill's second-wave understanding of "*what I feel is quite strongly a feminist position*" to what one might rephrase as "what I feel is quite strongly the *loss* of a feminist position." ... Kane is representative of the 1990s "woman" playwright who is genealogically connected to feminist theatre histories, but is generationally divorced from an "old" style of feminist attachment. [*Blasted*] figures the fault line between a "personal as political feminist past" and a "personal without a feminist political present/future." (580)

In her cogent, sometimes bleak analysis of what Jill Dolan might call the state of "what is" for feminist artists and scholars today, Aston addresses the feminist performance community with this question: if our shared present is not so much "post-feminist" as it is lost-feminist, and if the women practising feminism today do so from within a variety of competing political frameworks that may not easily permit that fraught term entry, how might feminist performance theorists and practitioners account for the divide between word and action – being and doing – that has taken such deep root around us? Can we articulate a feminist politics *of doing* on the stage that also accounts for feminism's losses? Might that shift begin to transform the loss of feminist feeling into a fresh hope, source of pleasure and site of feminist political aspiration for the future?

Case study 3: *How to Become a Cupcake*, The Famous Lauren Barri Holstein (2013)

In her "complete history of feminism" posted on *feminist-times.com* in October 2013, American-born, London-based, Jewish performance artist The Famous Lauren Barri Holstein describes the beginning of the feminist movement like this:

> Ok so obviously the first thing that ever hap-
> pened in the history of the world is that Eve, the
> "Spare Rib," really wanted to do it with Adam,
> so she convinced him to eat the pregnant seedy
> pomegranate juicy vagina fruit, so that he'd real-
> ize that what he really wanted to eat was Eve's
> luscious seedy, juicy vag. It worked! Good job,
> Eve. You get yours!

Lauren Barri Holstein ("The Famous" is her performance persona) is well aware that things didn't turn out especially well for the Bible's Eve, of course: that's her point. Her take on Eve in this satirical history describes the archetypal Christian woman as agent of her own, sexy, fallen destiny because that's exactly what post-feminism demands of young women: that they claim their sexuality as power, identify as sexual agents in all (even potentially unpleasant) sexual situations and look up to gorgeous but powerful (powerful *because* gorgeous) women in the pop music industry, Hollywood and on social media – all the while trying to ignore the nagging feeling that they, themselves, aren't quite as empowered, as independent or even as safe as their diva avatars are made out to be online and on TV.

Holstein's practice is devoted to showcasing what happens to young female bodies torn physically as well as emotionally between a historical feminism that sought to empower them, and a contemporary, "post-feminist" popular culture in which such empowerment is available only to female bodies made sexually attractive in depressingly conventional ways. Her major productions *Splat!* and *How to Become a Cupcake/The Famous's Adaptation of Frankenstein* (both 2013) take place in the space feminism's loss opens up; they stage post-feminism's vaunted "girl power" as gloriously messy, physically draining and ultimately deeply dissatisfying. Holstein celebrates, glorifies, punishes and desecrates her explicitly sexualized body on stage in a series of self-contradictory performance actions that work to expose the contradictions buried within "girl power" itself. Speaking to Debbie Kilbride for BBC Radio 4's *Woman's Hour* in March 2013, Holstein described the sexual objectification of women's bodies as part of a "shared" cultural history, and noted that her "biggest question" as both an artist and a scholar of feminist performance is whether or not it is even possible for a "displayed" woman's body (on stage or elsewhere in the public sphere) to "have power" – expressing her kinship with the work of Peggy Phelan, among other early feminist performance theorists.

Holstein also, however, takes enormous pleasure in the diva persona she wears and the "feminist-lite" images she creates on stage, and this pleasure forms a significant part of her politics. She makes and unmakes the images of "hot" girl power in a detritus-strewn space, half naked and covered in all manner of stuff. She urinates on stage and pulls everything from knives, food and plastic toys from her vagina in full view of her audiences, with plenty of help from other supporting artists (none of whom are disguised backstage, or dressed in stagehand blacks – their labour is fully acknowledged). She sings along badly, and dances through her fatigue, to contemporary torch songs by boy bands and female divas like Katy Perry. With her characteristic sexy-gross mash-up Holstein "does" contemporary populist feminism as a confusing mess, a suite of intractable paradoxes and physically degrading actions, generating for her audiences a fierce parody of "what (neoliberal) women want" that is also a raucous demonstration of how much cheesy, seductive fun the spectacle of that "want" can be.

How to Become a Cupcake features Holstein and fellow artists Hrafnhildur Benediktsdóttir, Krista Vuori, Rebecca Duschl, Lucy McCormick, Christopher Matthew Hutchings, Amanda Prince-Lubawy and Katerina Paranama dressed in bright, cheap tutus, black bras and tank tops. Styled as an adaptation of *Frankenstein*, the show is framed around a series of "becomings" set to a Top 40 soundtrack as Holstein transforms into various food items associated with sexual play. (All of my descriptions of actions from *How to Become a Cupcake* are drawn from videos freely available on the sharing site Vimeo, although the complete video of the show is available for purchase through www.thefamousomg.com.) Holstein sprays shot after shot of aerosol whipped cream into her mouth, dribbling and spitting each onto the stage floor in order to make room for more. She inserts a stick of cotton candy into her vagina, "fluffing" it from an awkward, upside-down angle before gingerly removing it. She offers a heartfelt lip-sync to the Backstreet Boys' *Incomplete* while one of her assisting artists fingers a jam donut and squeezes its contents into the mesh fabric of one of the cast's tutus. Wearing a shiny purple wig in homage to Katy Perry, Holstein dance-thrusts her chest and pelvis, with increasing speed and urgency, to *California Gurls* while (struggling) to suck her way through a mango. (Her moves become more erratic as the song progresses and the challenge of "hot" dancing catches up to the impossibility of "hot" mango-eating.) Finally, in a climactic number that begins as a lame-looking, half-hearted canteen food fight (perhaps in homage to food and pillow fights familiar from soft-core internet porn), Holstein is attacked by her crew with leftover bits of cream, donut and other half-eaten items before she launches into a ballet dance choreographed to the Backstreet Boys power ballad *I Want It That Way*. Her assistants, having recently cleaned up the stage, now assault her afresh with cans of whipped cream, hounding her like paparazzi. Unlike in the Katy Perry number, this time Holstein holds her line, rolling her hips and touching her cream-covered hair and breasts to the beat while the others crowd around her, shaking their cans and spraying her head with blunt, expressionless focus. The stage becomes a slippery mess; the audience laughs, applauds and hoots while Holstein fights to maintain her perfect form amid the cream on the floor and the other bodies in her way. It's hard work, and she looks utterly ridiculous (and profoundly unsexy) as she tries to master it.

Holstein has argued that she does not take either side in the post-feminist debate (Kilbride): she argues that she uses her performances to ask what it really means for ordinary young women that pop icons like Katy Perry or Britney Spears or Beyoncé, styled as all-powerful "hot chicks" by print and online media, can ostensibly make choices about their bodies, their sexuality and the display of both across the public sphere. Does this freedom of "the hot and famous" represent any kind of real power for girls and women not similarly privileged? Or is this another example of neoliberal exceptionalism, in which select women are represented as the embodiment of "having it all" – evidence of feminism as having "won" – while the rest of us struggle to make sense of why we don't feel better about the shapes of our bodies or more secure about the options available for our futures? Although Holstein claims not to have an answer, *How to Become a Cupcake* ultimately reveals exactly that feeling of *not better* as Holstein and her team share with us the fraught feelings that follow the moment the power ballad ends and the spectacular singing-dancing body disappears from view.

Unlike the perfectly preened and carefully framed pop divas on TV, "The Famous" female body never leaves her stage. Instead, as her singing and dancing ends, Holstein drops her plastic smile and owns the aerosol-cream-covered, dripping, grunting, heaving, sweating mess of her body. She becomes, in fact, exactly the kind of body that Young Jean Lee offers to startled spectators in *Untitled Feminist Show*. When the pop hits aren't playing, the sound tech turns the soundtrack off; we hear the cue, and then we hear the squelching of feet on wet stage floors, the sounds of Holstein catching her breath, drinking water, wading through the literal heap of crap around her. The sounds of bodies at work fill our ears. She and her crew move around the space, looking for the next set of props, the next part of the script; they ask the backstage crew to change sound or lights, get set up for the next spectacle of powerful girly-womanhood. At one point captured in a stand-alone video on her Vimeo site, (titled "Cupcake/Frankenstein – Splat! is better") Holstein sits nearly naked, wet and small in the middle of the stage, and declares into the microphone that *How to Become a Cupcake* is really "a piece of shit," worthless, embarrassing. My feminist spectator's ears prick up: I hear in her voice the exhaustion, disillusionment, even the sense of defeat that are the by-products of creating the sexy-dirty images of girl-power fame-and-fortune around which the show is built. I'm reminded of Hattie Morahan's rendering of Ibsen's carefully put-together Nora Helmer as the hard physical and emotional labour that goes into becoming the "cupcake" – the empowered woman who no longer needs the help of feminism – shines into view.

Conclusion: on ageing

Lauren Barri Holstein, like Debbie Tucker Green and the late Sarah Kane, is a next-generation feminist artist whose work explores the sometimes-turbulent emotions feminism brings up for young men and women today. Her spectacles of sexy pseudo-empowerment offer one powerful response to the losses that structure our so-called post-feminist present, from a young artist still navigating the demands that present makes on her body and her politics. Holstein's messy, complicated approach to feminist performance art is welcome, but it is not new; her practice harks back to that of foundational artists such as Carolee Schneeman and Yoko Ono, among many others. These artists, along with the scholars who shaped our understanding of their and other foundational feminist theatre work, are now growing older and more physically vulnerable, and their ageing is having an important impact on the direction feminist performance theory and criticism will take in the years to come. In an essay published in Farfan and Ferris's recent collection *Contemporary Women Playwrights*, Elin Diamond revisits three of the artists – Deb Margolin, Peggy Shaw and Robbie McCauley – about whom she wrote in *Unmaking Mimesis*. In her introduction Diamond says that Margolin, Shaw and McCauley's newest performance works are "bringing us news of their aging bodies," and particularly news of how older feminist bodies navigate the "biopolitics of medical science" (258), which remains dominated by powerful, self-assured men. Like Dolan and Aston, Diamond uses affect theory as her critical framework for this essay, and throughout she argues that today's frontier of feminist theatre theory may lie at the junction of her older, "gestic" feminist model and models of spectatorship that take the emotional connections made between feminist performers and feminist spectators more fully into account.

Peggy Shaw's latest solo work, *Ruff* (2012), illustrates perfectly, and movingly, how this new, hybrid model of "feminist performance affect" might look and feel. Shaw is a founding member of the WOW Café, the New York performance space that had such a profound influence on early feminist performance theory, and she has been active as a solo artist as well as a collaborator with Spiderwoman Theatre, Hot Peaches and Split Britches since the 1970s. In 2011, Shaw suffered a stroke; it changed the way her brain works and altered the ways in which her body copes with the rigours of making art, learning lines, performing and touring. But it did not stop her. *Ruff*, which Shaw devised with her long-time artistic partner Lois Weaver, is all about the experience of living and working with her stroke-changed body and mind. The performance premiered in Alaska late in 2012, and visited Dixon Place in New York in early 2013 before coming to the Chelsea Theatre in London for two days in April, where I saw it. *Ruff* is, in Alena Dierickx's words, an "ode to vulnerability and ageing that is all too often hidden away as if it is shameful or, worse still, boring" – especially as that vulnerability and ageing affect women's bodies and their portrayal in popular culture.

Older women – like feminism itself – are having a "moment" as I write this: popular British actors Helen Mirren (currently aged 69), Charlotte Rampling (currently 68) and Tilda Swinton (currently 53) have just signed contracts to represent cosmetics firms L'Oréal Paris and Nars for campaigns in 2014 and 2015 (Marriott). Their airbrushed images appear everywhere, representing ageing female bodies as beautiful, sexy and – of course – powerful. But just as not all young women can "own" their bodies as Beyoncé or Katy Perry can, not all older women's bodies fit this sexy/powerful mould: fear, confusion and a loss of independence are all hallmarks of getting older, and together they place many older women especially at risk. Shaw's willingness to make theatre from and about this risk is exactly what makes *Ruff* an essential intervention into the history of feminist performance theory and practice now.

The night I saw *Ruff*, Shaw arrived on stage to thunderous applause and hoots of glee from an audience of friends and fans; she grinned broadly, clutching an orange, a shoe and a bottle of water. When the applause died down she began speaking in a quite formal, studied tone – almost as though she couldn't remember her lines. I became anxious; this wasn't the virtuoso performer I remembered from earlier shows like *Dress Suits to Hire* (1987) or *Menopausal Gentleman* (1997). She was unmistakably an older, physically weaker woman. I watched, uncomfortable, as she struggled to hang in there.

Then, with her trademark killer timing, she handed me her orange.

"Will you hold my orange, please?" The line was completely sincere; as she delivered it Shaw looked straight into my eyes and asked me directly to share my physical space with her new, awkward presence. I panicked briefly, took the orange and then sat back in my chair, cradling it in both hands. I didn't know what to do with it, or how long I would have to hold it. But I felt a very strong surge of responsibility towards it: I knew I could not put it down, like a bag or a coat or whatever else I had brought with me. It wasn't *stuff*; it was a kind of connective tissue, maybe scar tissue, and it linked me to this performer who needed me (Diamond, "Deb Margolin" 271). Next, Shaw gave my friend Catherine Silverstone the shoe she was holding, and then our friend Lara Shalson her bottle of water. Always with the same question: could you please…? And just like that, we were all in it, with her, together. Shaw's need for some people to help her hold her stuff had sutured us into a small community of feminist spectators: a community of shared feeling, a community of shared purpose and commitment to one another.

I remained nervous for about 10 minutes as Shaw laboured to get into the show's rhythm. It was then that I realized she was actually making *Ruff* out of these strange moments of intense awkwardness, placing both her damaged body as well as her cognitive instability audaciously on display. Three LCD monitors on wheels scrolled the full text of the show so that Shaw could turn to any one of them at any moment and catch up with herself. She sat whenever she needed to, took a break when she needed to, and drank from the bottle of water when she felt a cough coming on – though only after first asking Lara, politely, if she might have a drink.

Ruff is not a performance in which Shaw *only seems* not to be in control; it is a show about the experience, and the implications, of losing control: of her body, of her independence, of the woman she had been. It asks us to consider what that loss means for her as a performance maker, a sexual being, an older woman, a human being. But *Ruff* is also a show about its audiences of feminist spectators, and about the work that still needs *our* doing. In *Ruff*, Shaw casts us as her caregivers, asks for our renewed commitment to feminist community, because without that community she might, literally, pass away from us. I hold the orange; I witness Shaw's repeated memory breaks and recoveries; I watch her patiently as she sits, then lies down; I am ready to help her up if need be. In each of these moments I am invited to act – must act, am compelled by our shared vulnerability, as both women and human beings, to act – as part of Shaw's support system. It feels good.

Ruff stages a portrait of a strong, able, funny and beautiful feminist performance artist in transition. In this, and despite the age difference between Shaw and Holstein, it lies not so far removed from *How to Become a Cupcake*, nor from Nora's monumental decision to cross her husband's threshold in *A Doll's House*, nor from the power and the risk involved in mounting the stage, naked and exposed, in *Untitled Feminist Show*. The theory, the plays, the artists and the scholars I have written about in *Theatre & Feminism* share in common the work of making, managing and thriving through transitions of all kinds. As women's living and working conditions have evolved over the last several decades, the work of feminist performance theory and criticism has tracked those evolutions across the stage and emboldened feminist spectators to read, understand, critique and rejoice in what they have seen of their lives shifting and changing before the footlights. Now, as Brechtian techniques and a focus on the gaze give way to a focus on the feelings of hope, loss, fear and shame that shape women's lives, separately and together, under neoliberal globalization, Feminist performance scholarship and practice continue to provide spaces where women of all ages and backgrounds can come together to dream of a better, fairer world for all.

further reading

Throughout this book I have emphasized major trends in feminist performance theory and criticism since 1975, with a focus on the Anglo-American context. Here, I would like to recommend further reading by scholars working in or on other parts of the globe; by those working intersectionally on issues of gender, race, cultural and/or sexual identity; as well as some very recent work by the pioneering women who have featured in the previous pages.

Much contemporary feminist work is intersectional: it accounts for feminist issues in relation to issues of race, social class, sexual orientation and economics so extensively that often the best scholars writing on feminist topics today are not, in name, "feminist" exclusively. Three award-winning critics who work in this way are Sara Warner at Cornell University, Brandi Wilkins Catanese at the University of California, Berkeley and Alicia Arrizón at the University of California, Riverside. Warner's *Acts of Gaiety: LGBT Performance and the Politics of Pleasure* (University of Michigan Press, 2012) explores the intersections of pleasurable feelings and political activism in a wide range of queer performance, and especially lesbian performance; she flexes her activist muscles on behalf of socially marginalized women in her shorter piece, "The Medea Project: Mythic Theater for Incarcerated Women," published in *Feminist Studies in summer* (2004). Like *Acts of Gaiety*, Catanese's *The Problem of the Color[blind]: Racial Transgression and the Politics of Black Performance* (University of Michigan Press, 2011) is a multi-award-winning book; it bridges feminist performance theory and criticism, African American studies and cultural history as it considers the relationships between race and gender in casting decisions and other practical performance considerations, both at the theatre and in Hollywood. Arrizón's work, driven in part by her personal experience growing up on the US/Mexico border, blends an interest in Latina/o identity, transculturalism, queer studies and feminist theory; her *Queering Mestizaje: Transculturation and Performance* was published by the University of Michigan Press in 2006.

South Asia has been at the epicentre of outstanding feminist performance scholarship in the past decade, particularly as critics explore legacies of partition and the potential impact of global neoliberalism on the subcontinent's female populations. Deepti Misri's *Beyond Partition: Gender, Violence, and Representation in Postcolonial India* (University of Illinois Press, 2014) considers the many ways in which state violence intersects with gendered violence, and accounts for both women's and men's experiences in the process. Bishnupriya Dutt and Urmimala Sarkar Munsi's *Engendering Performance: Indian Women Performers in Search of an Identity* (Sage, 2010) examines the work of actresses alongside the work of female dancers during the transition from the colonial to the post-colonial periods in India. Fawzia Afsal-Kahn's "Pakistani Muslim Theatre at Home and Abroad: A Critical Manifesto for a Feminist Home-Coming" (in Aston and Case's *Staging International Feminisms*, Palgrave, 2007) and Kanika Batra's *Feminist Visions and Queer Futures in Postcolonial Drama: Community, Kinship, and Citizenship* (Routledge, 2011) extend their lenses beyond India to look at feminist and queer theatre in Pakistan, Nigeria and Jamaica as well. (My thanks to Manolagayatri Kumarswamy for introducing me to several of these titles.)

Feminist scholars often do not work where they were raised; they are world travellers, bringing their personal experiences along with their professional expertise to careers across the globe. From a Japanese perspective and a British base (at Birkbeck, University of London), Nobuko Anan writes contemporary feminist histories of popular Japanese performance; her "*The Rose of Versailles*: Women and Revolution in Girls' Manga and the Socialist Movement in Japan" appears in the February 2014 issue of *The Journal of Popular Culture*. At Georgetown University, German feminist performance critic Katrin Sieg writes at the inter-sections of German theatre, feminism, and neoliberal politics in pieces such as "Globalizing Neoliberalism, Travelling Feminisms: Pollesch@Prater" (in *Staging International*

Feminisms). Galway native Emer O'Toole is now based at Concordia University in Montreal; she writes thoughtfully but also playfully about the way we perform our genders today in her *Girls Will Be Girls: Dressing Up, Playing Parts, and Daring to Act Differently* (Orion, 2015). Others write and teach where they grew or studied, returning home to rebuild old attitudes and expectations: Melissa Sihra's *Women in Irish Drama: A Century of Authorship and Representation* (Palgrave, 2007) collects essays by top Irish feminist scholars working on theatre and performance, while Miriam Haughton and Maria Kurdi's *Radical Contemporary Theatre Practices by Women in Ireland* (Carysfort Press, 2015) pushes the discussion towards the next generation.

Many of the most influential performance scholars of the twentieth century continue to publish today, and their latest work stands tall among the best new writing in the field. Heartfelt and accessible, Elaine Aston and Geraldine Harris's *A Good Night Out for the Girls: Popular Feminisms in Contemporary Theatre and Performance* (Palgrave, 2012) follows Dolan and Chansky as it takes seriously populist women's theatrical entertainments in contemporary Britain; meanwhile, Aston's "But Not That: Caryl Churchill's Political Shape Shifting at the Turn of the Millennium," published in the journal *Modern Drama* in 2013, challenges critical orthodoxy as it argues for Caryl Churchill's turn away from Bertolt Brecht in recent years – and towards a different, more felt form of feminist politics. Dolan's blog is now a book, *The Feminist Spectator in Action* (Palgrave, 2013), and like its web-based namesake it is written with a wide, non-scholarly audience in mind, designed to make its politics accessible and intended to provoke positive debate about representations of gender in the public sphere. Finally: Sue-Ellen Case's *Feminism and Theatre*, the book to which *this* book owes its inspiration, was reissued in 2008 by Palgrave, with a forward by Elaine Aston. I urge you to check it out.

Aston, Elaine. "Feeling the Loss of Feminism: Sarah Kane's *Blasted* and an Experiential Genealogy of Contemporary Women's Playwriting." *Theatre Journal* 62.4 (2010): 575–91.

———. "Room for Realism." Unpublished Conference Paper. *IFTR Annual Conference*, Barcelona, July 2013. Lecture.

Aston, Elaine, and Geraldine Harris. *A Good Night Out for the Girls: Popular Feminisms in Contemporary Theatre and Performance.* Basingstoke: Palgrave Macmillan, 2012.

Aston, Elaine, and Sue-Ellen Case, eds. *Staging International Feminisms.* Basingstoke: Palgrave Macmillan, 2007.

Barker, Roberta. *Early Modern Tragedy, Gender and Performance, 1984–2000: The Destined Livery.* Basingstoke: Palgrave Macmillan, 2007.

Bates, Laura. *Everyday Sexism.* New York: Simon and Schuster, 2014.

Burton, Rebecca. *Adding It Up: The Status of Women in Canadian Theatre.* Toronto: Nightwood Theatre and Playwrights Guild of Canada, 2006.

Butler, Judith. *Bodies That Matter: On the Discursive Limits of "Sex."* London: Routledge, 1993.

———. *Gender Trouble: Feminism and the Subversion of Identity.* New York: Routledge, 1990.

———. "Performative Acts and Gender Constitution: An Essay in Phenomenology and Feminist Theory." *Theatre Journal* 40.4 (1988): 519–31.

———. *Precarious Life: The Powers of Mourning and Violence.* London: Verso, 2004.

Carnicke, Sharon Marie. *Stanislavsky in Focus: An Acting Master for the Twenty-First Century.* 2nd ed. London: Routledge, 2008.

Case, Sue-Ellen. *Feminism and Theatre*. London: Routledge, 1988.

————, ed. *Performing Feminisms: Feminist Critical Theory and Theatre*. Baltimore, MD: Johns Hopkins University Press, 1990.

Catanese, Brandi Wilkins. "Taking the Long View." *Theatre Journal* 62.4 (2010): 547–51.

Chansky, Dorothy. "Usable Performance Feminism for Our Time: Reconsidering Betty Friedan." *Theatre Journal* 60.3 (2008): 341–64.

Churchill, Caryl. *Top Girls*. Student ed. London: Methuen Drama, 1991.

Cima, Gay Gibson. *Performing Women: Female Characters, Male Playwrights, and the Modern Stage*. Ithaca, NY: Cornell University Press, 1993.

Cohen, Patricia. "Rethinking Gender Bias in Theater." *New York Times* 23 June 2009. Web. 5 February 2015.

Cosslett, Rhiannon Lucy, and Holly Baxter. *The Vagenda: A Zero Tolerance Guide to the Media*. New York: Random House, 2014.

Cracknell, Carrie, dir. *A Doll's House*. By Henrik Ibsen. Perf. Hattie Morahan, Dominic Rowan. Young Vic Theatre, London. 2012. Performance.

Cracknell, Carrie, and Nick Payne. *Nora: A Short Film Responding to Ibsen's A Doll's House*. 18 October 2012. Theguardian.com. Web. 5 February 2015.

Davy, Kate. *Lady Dicks and Lesbian Brothers: Staging the Unimaginable at the WOW Café Theatre*. Ann Arbor: University of Michigan Press, 2010.

Diamond, Elin. "Brechtian Theory/Feminist Theory: Toward a Gestic Feminist Criticism." *TDR* 32.1 (1988): 82–94.

————. "Deb Margolin, Robbie McCauley, Peggy Shaw: Affect and Performance." In *Contemporary Women Playwrights: Into the Twenty-First Century*. Ed. Penny Farfan and Lesley Ferris. Basingstoke: Palgrave Macmillan, 2014. 258–74.

————. *Unmaking Mimesis: Essays on Feminism and Theater*. London: Routledge, 1997.

Dolan, Jill. "Feminist Performance Criticism and the Popular: Reviewing Wendy Wasserstein." *Theatre Journal* 60.3 (2008): 433–57.

————. *The Feminist Spectator as Critic*. Ann Arbor: University of Michigan Press, 1988.

————. *Utopia in Performance: Finding Hope at the Theater*. Ann Arbor: University of Michigan Press, 2005.

Farfan, Penny, and Lesley Ferris, eds. *Contemporary Women Playwrights: Into the Twenty-First Century*. Basingstoke: Palgrave Macmillan, 2014.

Finley, Karen, and Richard Schechner. "A Constant State of Becoming: An Interview." *TDR* 32.1 (1988): 152–8.

Foucault, Michel. *Discipline and Punish: The Birth of the Prison*. 1975. New York: Vintage, 1995.

Freud, Sigmund. "Three Essays on the Theory of Sexuality." 1905. In *The Standard Edition of the Complete Psychological Works of Sigmund Freud*. Vol. 7. Ed. James Strachey with Anna Freud. London: Hogarth Press, 1986. 123–254.

Gay, Roxane. *Bad Feminist: Essays*. New York: HarperCollins, 2014.

Glassberg Sands, Emily. "Opening the Curtain on Playwright Gender: An Integrated Economic Analysis of Discrimination in American Theatre." MA diss., Princeton University, 2009.

Goodman, Lizbeth. *Contemporary Feminist Theatres: To Each Her Own*. London: Routledge, 1993.

Harris, Geraldine, and Elaine Aston. *Feminist Futures? Theatre, Performance, Theory*. Basingstoke: Palgrave Macmillan, 2006.

Hart, Lynda, ed. *Making a Spectacle: Feminist Essays on Contemporary Women's Theatre*. Ann Arbor: University of Michigan Press, 1989.

Hart, Lynda, and Peggy Phelan, eds. *Acting Out: Feminist Performances*. Ann Arbor: University of Michigan Press, 1993.

Harvey, David. *A Brief History of Neoliberalism*. London: Oxford University Press, 2005.

Holland, Sharon. In "A Forum on Theatre and Tragedy: A Response to September 11, 2001." *Theatre Journal* 54.1 (2002): 95–138 (118–19).

Holman, Rebecca. "'I've Had Death and Rape Threats Simply for Starting the Conversation about Everyday Sexism': Laura Bates on Trolls, Lad Culture, and the Future of Everyday Sexism." *The Debrief* 30 April 2014. Web. 5 February 2015.

Holstein, Lauren Barrie. "The Complete History of Feminism, According to the Famous Lauren Barrie Holstein." *Feminist Times* 17 October 2013. Feministtimes.com. Web. 5 February 2015.

———. *How to Become a Cupcake*. 2013. Vimeo.com. Web. 5 February 2015.

Kilbride, Debbie. "Interview with The Famous Lauren Barrie Holstein." *Woman's Hour* 27 March 2013. BBC.co.uk. Web. 5 February 2015.

Lampe, Eelka. "Rachel Rosenthal: Creating Her Selves." *TDR* 32.1 (1988): 170–90.

Lee, Young Jean. *Untitled Feminist Show*. Perf. Becca Blackwell, Katy Pyle, Desiree Burch, Lady Rizo, Madison Krekel, and Jen Rosenblit. Harbourfront Centre, Toronto. 2012. Performance.

Malague, Rosemary. *An Actress Prepares: Women and 'The Method'*. London: Routledge, 2012.

McRobbie, Angela. "Top Girls? Young Women and the Postfeminist Sexual Contract." *Cultural Studies* 21.4–5 (2007): 718–37.

Morahan, Hattie. Personal Interview. London, June 2014.

Moran, Caitlin. *How to Be a Woman*. New York: Random House, 2012.

Mulvey, Laura. "Visual Pleasure and Narrative Cinema." *Screen* 16.3 (1975): 6–18.

Pabón, Jessica N. "Be About It: Graffiteras Performing Feminist Community." *TDR* 57.3 (2013): 88–116.

Perkins, Kathy A., and Sandra L. Richards. "Black Women Playwrights in American Theatre." *Theatre Journal* 62.4 (2010): 541–5.

Phelan, Peggy. "Feminist Theory, Poststructuralism, and Performance." *TDR* 32.1 (1988): 107–27.

———. *Unmarked: The Politics of Performance*. London: Routledge, 1993.

"Postfeminism." *Wikipedia: The Free Encyclopedia*. Wikipedia.org. Web. 30 March 2015.

Reinelt, Janelle. "Beyond Brecht: Britain's New Feminist Drama." *Theatre Journal* 38.2 (1986): 154–63.

Ryan, Erin Gloria. "Goodbye and Good Riddance, Angry Little Men Who Hate Skyler White." *Jezebel.com* 30 September 2013. Web. 5 February 2015.

Saunders, Graham. *Love Me or Kill Me: Sarah Kane and the Theatre of Extremes*. Manchester: Manchester University Press, 2002.

Shaw, Peggy. *Ruff*. Devised with Lois Weaver. Perf. Peggy Shaw. 2012. Chelsea Theatre, London. 4 April 2013. Performance.

Shevtsova, Maria. "On Directing: A Conversation with Katie Mitchell." *New Theatre Quarterly* 22.1 (2006): 3–18.

Solga, Kim. "Mother Courage and its Abject: Reading the Violence of Identification." *Modern Drama* 46.3 (2003): 339–57.

Solomon, Alisa. *Re-Dressing the Canon: Essays on Theater and Gender*. London: Routledge, 1997.

Stanislavski, Konstantin. *An Actor's Work: A Student's Diary*. Trans. Jean
    Benedetti. London: Routledge, 2008.
"Untitled Feminist Show." Young Jean Lee's Theater Company.
    youngjeanlee.org. Web. 16 June 2015.
Wente, Margaret. "Women Against #womenagainstfeminism." *Globe and
    Mail* 9 August 2014. Web. 5 February 2015.

index

acknowledgements

For Sue-Ellen Case,
author of the original *Feminism and Theatre* (1988);

For Jen Harvie and Susan Bennett,
cherished mentors, colleagues and friends;

And for all of the pioneering women scholars
(Elaine, Elin, Janelle, Jill, Peggy and so many more)
whose examples nurture my own work
and give this book life.

Fierce gratitude!